OPEN UNIVERSITIES

OPEN UNIVERSITIES
Modern Educational Innovations

P. Satyanarayana
Lakshmi Mantha
Emmanuel DK Meduri

SHIPRA

ISBN: 978-81-7541-843-1

First Published in India in 2016

Open Universities: Modern Educational Innovations

Published by:
SHIPRA PUBLICATIONS
LG 18-19, Pankaj Central Market, I.P. Ext.
Patparganj, Delhi-110092, India
Tel: 91-11-2223 5152, 2223 6152
E-mail: info@shiprapublication.com
www.shiprapublication.com

Contents

JOURNEY OF OPEN UNIVERSITIES

PROFILES OF POPULAR OPEN UNIVERSITIES

KEY AREAS OF OPEN UNIVERSITIES

Journey of Open Universities

1

Genesis and Growth of Open Universities

Open universities revolutionised lifelong learning in many countries. These institutions are inspired by democratization, growing demands for tertiary education, technological developments well suited to mass education, and the human resource needs of modern societies. Open universities have been a great success, by several indicators, in most countries where they have been established. They have the evidence of high quality instruction. Open universities probably will go down in the history books as one of the most important educational innovations of the 20th century. They have instilled hope and made it a reality. They have become popular national resources.

The term 'Open University' can be interpreted multidimensionally. Van dem Boom and Schlusmans showed these dimensions clearly in their study *Didactics of Open Education—Background, Analysis and Approaches.* They show what advocates of open learning understand by the term 'Open University'. They combine the term with the following expectations and demands:

- university education is to be made less expensive;
- more people are to be enabled to take part in cultural life;
- the overcrowded traditional universities are to be relieved;
- new groups of students are to be formed;
- the further democratization of society is to be supported by enabling more people to study while working, thus making the world in which they live more transparent to them and empowering them to act autonomously;
- lifelong learning, which has been propagated for decades, is to receive better opportunities for realisation; and
- additional chances and further impetus are to be provided for people to gain more qualifications, so as to enable them to survive in today's employment world.

From the point view of university distance teaching pedagogies the open university has played a pioneering role because it established a form of studying that had never been seen in the world. This was achieved through a series of innovations. Their integrated interplay in a new teaching and learning system achieved an enormous innovative thrust that adapted distance education consistently to changed technologies and social requirements and thus received worldwide notice (Otto Peters).

The open university has developed ways of thinking and working and strategies for teaching and learning that have never been achieved so radically and consistently by any other university.

The establishment of the Open University in the United Kingdom in 1969 and the subsequent foundation of similar systems in other parts of the World created a revolution by making higher education more accessible and less costly. The foundation of the Open University in the United Kingdom marked the beginning of a new and prestigious era in the history of distance education. Till 1969 educationists and educational planners in several countries were sceptical in their estimate of distance teaching institutions. The establishment of a State funded University adopting distance teaching methods changed the situation. The methods used by these institutions to instruct their students varied substantially from country to country but all are dedicated to the sole aim of opening up the world of higher education. The Open University of the United Kingdom (UKOU) started a new era of distance education and it has set new standards ever since.

The UKOU set out from its inception to achieve parity of standards with conventional universities in Britain. Jennie Lee, the Minister assigned responsibility for the UKOU project, was adamant that it should have the highest academic status. She scrapped the proposals that had been worked out within the British Department of Education and Science for an experimental college of the Air and pushed forward her own ideas: "The University of Air was to be an independent university, offering its own degrees, making no compromise whatever on standards and offering an opportunity to all, without entrance qualification."

The University, once established, accepted the challenge. "Our task was to provide courses that would lead to first degrees equivalent in standard to those of any other British first degree."

Perry describes the foundation of the UKOU as:

> "...an act of faith that was remarkable and almost miraculous. The decision was received with scepticism, indeed with scorn and ridicule, by virtually the whole of the academic establishment, by almost the whole of the academic establishment, by almost the whole of the national press and by at least half the political world. And the biggest cause of that scepticism was the belief in academic circles that higher education was critically dependent on face-to-face tuition."

In Germany the Fern Universitat undertook the even more daunting task of achieving degrees that would be interchangeable, both during the study programmes and when awarded with the degrees of the conventional German universities.

Open universities have had to establish a reputation for reliability, validity and credibility. Neil said that to succeed that had to:

- create and produce learning materials of exceptional quality.
- use well conceived teaching styles, teaching methods and student support services clearly designed to promote effective independent learning.
- design curricular manifestly relevant to specified and real needs of education.
- avoid excessive unorthodoxy or adventurousness, while maintaining aa prudently innovative approach to curriculum design.
- carefully evaluate student performance and consistently analyse and use feedback information to improve their systems.

The UKOU survived a change in government two years after its establishment and rapidly attracted wide international interest. By 1995, open universities of one kind or other had been setup in Canada, Germany, Israel, Pakistan, Spain and Thailand. The idea was adopted alike by secular democracies and fading autocracies. By late 1990s, there are over thirty open universities. Today there are over fifty open universities in the world.

Critical Issues in Policy and Planning

Now, many countries and provinces in the countries are keen to setup open universities. Distance education theorists and practitioners suggest the following critical issues in policy and planning for open universities:

- Identifying the target population and their needs.
- Choosing the type of system.
- Choosing the appropriate technology for delivery.
- Business planning and costing open university system.
- Materials development or acquiring.
- Tutoring and supporting students.
- Recruiting and enrolling students.
- Assessing students.
- Managing and administering the system.
- Monitoring, evaluating and quality assurance.

History

The idea of open university occurred to some individuals and institutions even before the establishment of the UKOU. Stuart Marriot discovered in an article published in *The University Extension Journal* in 1891:

> Before long some university will seize the unequalled opportunity ....Will broadly lay down a curriculum of study for degrees in new lines suited to the needs of those who desire to carry on their intellectual culture side by side with the regular business of life.

In an American radio magazine in 1922 appeared the words:

> The people's University of the Air will have a greater student body than all over universities put together.

In 1926 in England, J.C. Stobart, author of two reliable pieces of higher popular education, *The Glory that was Greece* and *The Grandeur that was Rome*, mooted something similar.

Historically, The University of South Africa is the first open university. The University of South Africa began as the University of the Cape of Good Hope in 1873 as an examining body for affiliated university colleges. In 1916 it was established as a Federation of Colleges. By the end of Second World War the colleges became autonomous and independent and the University slowly and gradually concentrated on external studies. In 1946 The University of South Africa became a teaching as well as an examining institution, the first public university in the World to teach exclusively by means of distance education.

In 1962 Michael Young proposed an open university to prepare people for external degrees of London University but his energies went into the establishment of National Extension College.

Emergence of Open University of United Kingdom (UKOU)

In 1963 two events occurred of some importance to the emergence of the UKOU. One was the publication of the Robbins Report on Higher Education, the Report of the Committee appointed in 1961 under the chairmanship of Lord Robbins to review the pattern full time higher education in Great Britain. The Robbins Committee did not make any firm suggestion for an institution like the open university, but it mentioned the potential value of 'the establishment by some universities of correspondence courses'. The second event of 1963 was the succession of Harold Wilson to the leadership of the Labour Party. Harold Wilson, before he became the leader of the Labour Party, was greatly impressed by the higher education in the USA. He saw the immense potential of television in every home. Harold Wilson also knew well the Soviet use of radio and correspondence courses for degree teaching. The influence of United States and Soviet Russia influenced Harold Wilson to conceive a vision in which television and radio would be used to bring higher education into every home in the UK. Harold Wilson outlined his scheme for a University of the Air in an election campaign speech in Glasgow in 1963. He envisaged this as a consortium of existing Universities using broadcasting and correspondence tuition to bring their teaching to adult students in their homes. When Labour Party came to power, Wilson handed over the responsibility for realising his dream to Jennie Lee, who was at the time Under Secretary of State for Education and Science. As the ideas developed, Jennie Lee made it clear that she wanted an autonomous, independent university equal to any other. She overcame the scepticism an even hostility of the educational establishment by 'outsnobbing the snobs', as she put it herself. She brought together a Planning Committee which included five Vice-Chancellors, the Principal of a Polytechnic, and the leaders of two education authorities. Their recommendations won the support of Jennie Lee's colleagues in the Cabinet, and the Open University at last became government policy, and shortly afterwards, a reality.

Perry (1986) the founder Vice-Chancellor of the UKOU, recalling the initial years of the University noted:

> Academics all over Britain accept that the Open University has succeeded, that distance learning works and that the Open University graduates are as good as any others. They (these graduates) have been accepted by every other British University in postgraduate courses without any question. The quality of the courses is seen and is commended by the academic world. The quality of the students, the quality of the exams—they are all recognised by the academics in other universities. But emotionally, many of them don't accept it all. Emotionally there still is a strong feeling that on-campus teaching in the face-to-face situation is the one way of actually teaching and that this is the vital thing in order to train scholars for the future. It may take decades rather than years to overcome the emotional reaction. You have to remember, I suppose, that every advance in education has been resisted for years and years. When we tried to introduce universal primary education, people argued that losing child labour out of coal mines would cause economic unrest. The same sort of people objected to universal secondary education because it was going to over-educate the working classes who ought to be kept in their place and learn a trade. I suppose the same reaction occurs to the idea of universal tertiary education or certainly the opportunity for it.

Open Universities without having the word 'Open'

There are certain open universities in the world without having the word 'open' in their titles. Examples include University of South Africa, Athabasca University, Payama Noor University, Universitias Terbuka. All the sixteen open universities in India have the word 'open' in their titles. When the first open university in India was established in 1982 at Hyderabad, many educationists could not clearly understand the meaning of the word 'open'.

Mega Universities

Open universities are more accessible and less costly. This is especially true of the mega-universities, which are defined by Sir John Daniel, the Former Vice-Chancellor of the UKOU as distance teaching universities with over 1,00,000 students in degree programmes.

There were ten such institutions when Jon Daniel first published his book *Mega Universities and Knowledge Media: Technology Strategies for Higher Education* in 1996.

In 1999 there were 11 such institutions enrolling about 3 million students between them. Today the number of mega universities has doubled and student enrolments have tripled and new mega universities are on the horizon.

The mega university experience, as a particular form of distance education practice, has gained a rich and extensive experience in both the highly industrialized and the developing regions of our world.

In many respects, the practice of distance education in the mega universities context is unique when compared to other forms of distance education and face-to-face higher education provision. Further, the mega university, as institution, has the most extensive experience in technology mediate learning. It is unique innovation in the higher education sphere with global relevance. In the words of John Daniel and Wayne Mackintosh 'the mega-university system, as one of the most important innovations in higher education of the 20thcentury, has successfully combined the challenges of access and quality in an approach that can be scaled up in ways that reduce cost without compromising the core social values of the university.

Mega Universities of the World in 1999

Name of the Institution	*Country*	*Founded*
China TV University System	China	1979
Center Nationald'Enseignement a Distance	France	1939
Indira Gandhi National Open University	India	1985
Universitaas Terbuka	Indonesia	1984
Payame Noor University	Iran	1987
Korea National Open University	Korea	1982
University of South Africa	South Africa	1873
Universidad Nacional de Education a Distance	Spain	1972
Sukhothai Thammathiraat Open University	Thailand	1978
Anadolu University	Turkey	1982
The Open University	UK	1969

These institutions have greatly increased access to higher education in their countries while at the same time lowering the costs of university education in dramatic fashion. Most of the mega-open universities teach each student for less than half of the average cost per student in the other universities of their countries. Furthermore, in most of the mega-universities student fees provide more than half of the budget of the institution. At a time when governments are finding it increasingly difficult to respond to all the financial demands made upon them, the success of the mega-universities in reducing the cost of higher education has important implications for public policy.

Openness

The word 'open' has many meanings. Perhaps, the most commonly used sense of 'open' has been the idea of creating opportunities for study for those debarred from it for whatever reasons, be it lack of formal educational attainments or shortage of vacancies, poverty, remoteness, employment or domestic necessities.

Its use in the title of currently most conspicuous example-the British Open University—was to some extent an afterthought. When the Labour party, then in opposition, first put forward the proposal in 1963 the title used was 'University of the Air', and this title was again used when the idea became government policy in 1964. It was changed to 'Open University' by the Planning Committee set up in 1967.

The change of name was not due to any substantial change in the initial concept, but rather to consideration of prudence and publicity. 'University of the Art' overemphasized the significance of the broadcast media in the learning system planned. Though their contribution was thought essential to attract and secure the adherence of a new student-body at which the universities aimed, a more important characteristic was the waiving of formal entry qualification and, as 'open' indicated this, the new title was adopted.

The 'openness' is the cardinal feature of the open universities. It is often said that the British Open University's "uniqueness lies not merely in its application of modern communication technology, but also in its philosophical concept of openness".

In what sense are open universities "open"? the following four characteristics are the ones most frequently citied:

- openness with regard to person, regardless of prior academic qualifications and without any entrance examination. Essentially it is the students, not the institute who controls the decision of enrolments.
- openness with regard to place (and sometimes pace) of study. While there may be centres or even residential summer schools, there is no central campus or specific time and place of study. While there may be voluntary study, every home can be a campus.
- openness with regard to studies, generally there are few required subjects and emphasis is placed on broad, studies, independent choice of courses and application of effort. Guided self-learning, not teaching, is the principal mode of instruction.
- openness with regard to completion, deferment, temporary discontinuation or termination of studies.

The 'open' of a open university (Dutch Open University) is well explained by Pierre Morin the following way:

- 'open' means that the Open University does not impose any formal admission requirements and does not demand any formal proof of preliminary knowledge, nor is there an entrance examination. Both before and during the learning process the students have to decide for themselves whether they are capable of studying successfully.
- 'open' also means that the students are allowed a great deal of freedom in planning their courses of study. Strictly speaking there are no fixed degree programmes as such. First, a student can study one or two courses separately. A course usually contains one or two modules, representing one or two hundred hours of study. Secondly, when the students have followed several courses and have passed the exams they can ask for a statement or dossier (dossioma, portfolio) all the courses they have completed. Thirdly, Open University can recognize a series of courses by conferring an Open University degree. Finally, the Open University has designed a number of combinations of courses in such a way that they lead to degrees which are equal or almost equal to certain degrees in higher vocational or university education. However, students remain free to choose their own path through that combination.

- A third form of openness is the students' freedom to choose their own pace of study. In principle, the students can start a course whenever they want, and the Open University holds several examinations in each subject every year.
- However, the students remain completely free to use those facilities in whichever way they choose. This means that openness in the fourth place allows the Open University to leave the students alone with the learning material, although they can always ask for advice and supervision at the study centres. The students themselves really decide where and how they study.

UK Open University's Openness

The first Chancellor of the UK Open University, the late Lord Crowther, in his address, after receiving The Royal Charter in 1969, said that the Open University would be open, not only as to entry, but as to place, as to method and as to ideas. His address is worth reproducing here:

- We are open first, as to people. Not for us the carefully regulated escalation from one educational level to next by which the traditional universities establish their criteria for admission. The first, and most urgent, task before us is to cater for the many thousands of people, fully capable of a higher education, who for one reason or another, do not get it, or do not get as much of it as they can turn to advantage or as they discover, sometimes too late, that they need. Only in recent years have we come to realize how many such people there are, and how large are the gaps in educational provision through which they can fall. The existing system, for all its expansion, misses and leaves aside a great unused reservoir of human talent and potential. Men and women drop out through failures in the system, through disadvantages of their environment, through mistakes of their own judgment, through sheer bad luck. There are our primary material. To them we offer a further opportunity.
- But if this were all, we could hardly call ourselves a University. This is not simply an educational rescue mission- though that is our first task, and we do not decry it. But we also aim wider and higher. Whenever there is an unprovided need for higher education, supplementing the existing provision, there is our constituency....

- The Open University is not the rival of the existing universities. It is designed to take over where they are compelled to leave off….
- We are open as to places. This University has no cloisters—a word meaning closed. Hardly even shall we have a campus. By a very happy chance, our only local habitation will be in the new city that is to bear two of the widest-ranging names in the history of English thought, Milton Keynes. But this is only where the tip of our toe touches ground. The rest of the University will be disembodied and airborne. From the start, it will flow all over the United Kingdom….
- We are open as to methods. We start, in dependence on, in grateful partnership with, the BBC. But already the development of technology is marching on, and I predict that before long actual broadcasting will form only a small part of the University's output. The world is caught in a Communications Revolution…. Every new form of human communication will be examined to see how it can be used to raise and broaden the level of human understanding….
- We are open, finally, to ideas. It has been said that there are two aspects of education, both necessary. One regards the individual human mind as a vessel of varying capacity, into which is to be poured as much as it will hold of the knowledge and experience by which human society lives and moves. This is the Martha of education—and we shall have plenty of these tasks to perform. But the Mary regards the human mind more as a fire that has to be set alight. That also we take as our ambition….

Combining the vision of openness with the methods of distance education most open universities adhere to the following principles of the UK open University:

- Any person can enrol, regardless of pervious education
- Study is done at home, work or anywhere the student chooses
- Course materials are developed by teams of experts
- Tutoring is provided by other specialists
- The enterprise is large scale, usually national in scope
- It enrols large numbers and enjoys economics of scale
- There are large investments, mostly from public funds
- A wide variety of technologies are used
- A highly integrated system combined with heavy investment results in high quality.

Reasons for Founding

The reasons for setting up open universities, according the Holmberg, are mainly:

- the need felt in many counties to increase the offer of university education in general;
- a realization that adults, with jobs, family and social commitments constituted a large group of prospective part-time university students;
- a wish to server both individuals and society by offering study opportunities to adults, particularly disadvantaged groups;
- the need found in many professions for further training at an advanced level;
- a wish to support educational innovation; and
- a belief in the feasibility of an economical use of educational resources by mediated teaching.

Essential Components for Starting the System

Erling Ljosa, the Norwegian distance educator, identified the major components that are essential for starting an open university system. These are:

1. A clear Mission for the organization.
2. The Profile of Programmes and Course Curriculum.
3. Teaching Strategies and Techniques.
4. Learning Materials and Resources.
5. Communication Interaction
6. Local Support Systems for Learners
7. Delivery Systems
8. The Tutorial Assistance
9. Staffing Infrastructure
10. Management and Administration

Main Features

Dhanaranjan, the former President of the Commonwealth of Learning, identified the following features of open universities.

- They aspire to balance inequalities between age, gender and social groups in terms of education access.
- They attempt to offer 'a second chance' to those who may have missed out an earlier opportunity.

- They provide efficient and speedy training for targeted groups.
- They expand the capacity for education in new areas
- They expand education beyond barriers of space and time.
- They develop multiple competencies through recurrent and continuing education.
- They allow for learning to take place parallel to work and social obligation.

Remarkable Similarity

Given the nature of their clients, products and community expectations, the major open universities have in some way or other developed very much like each other in their broad make up. If one were to examine the basis for this remarkable similarity, one would discover that (Dhanarajan).

- they look very much like an industrial organization geared towards production, delivery and support services but take education to where students are rather than the other way around;
- they attempt to be learner centred in their nature;
- they have a national presence;
- they rely on technology both new and old.;
- they have greater use for part-time staff especially in student support areas;
- they provide highly flexible learning arrangements;
- they conduct teaching and learning based on a complex and highly interdependent system; and
- they incur high up-front capital investment and more modest recurrent costs.

Whom do Universities Serve?

Many distance educators worked in this area to find out whom do open universities serve and Holmberg was one among them. According to him open universities provide educational opportunities at a distance for the following:

- School leavers who are qualified for traditional university entry but couldn't be admitted because of non-availability of places in traditional universities and colleges.
- Adults who desire to acquire university level qualification but couldn't apply for entry to a traditional university because they

- ➢ Lack education qualifications required for entry.
- ➢ Have family commitments, especially to young children which tie them to their home.
- ➢ Prefer to study independently.
- ➢ Live in institutions (e.g., the handicapped), which they are unable to leave.
- ➢ Are in full-time employment and can't or choose not to give up their jobs.

- Teachers, professional and manpower groups who require vocational training, professional updating and increased knowledge levels but couldn't be released from their employments to attend a campus based university or training college.
- Adults who wish to pursue lifelong opportunities (continuing education) unrelated to the pursuit of a degree level qualification.

Organisational Structure

Open universities with similar goals can be organised in different ways, reflecting philosophical, social, cultural, political, geographical, historical and technological differences of the countries. The research findings on organizational design point towards a continuous process of evolution of the structure as the scope of activities of the institution expands in terms of its concept as well as geographical coverage. Therefore, there is not one optimal structure design which would always serve a strategy with maximum efficiency and effectiveness. However, it would be advisable for an institutional planner to keep the following factors in mind while deciding about the institutional structure (Ram Reddy, 1987):

- it must encourage innovation on the part of academics, staff, students and all the other associates.
- it must serve the institutional objectives both in the short and long run.
- it must facilitate the institutional communication process both within and outside with various interest groups.
- it must contribute towards organizational climate by encouraging participation rather than isolation, between the various officials and academics, and between the institution and the outside world.

- it should facilitate decision making and various implementation processes.
- it must fulfil the aspiration for professional growth of officials and academics,, and
- it must provide for task role clarity for various agencies and top officials involved in the implementation. The stability of top-level leadership is also an essential requirement of the structuring process.

Several writers proposed model organizational structures of distance education system (Erdos, Singh, Dodds, Ram Reddy).

Staffing

There is no single right approach to the staffing pattern of open universities. Staffing pattern depends on the aims and objectives of the open university. Some open universities hire staff on part-time basis while some others would have staff on permanent full time basis. No standards are evolved for the staffing systems of open universities. Rumble listed some of the staffing categories found in large scale distance education systems, which by no means are exhaustive list:

1. General management
2. Materials development, production and presentation
3. Student administration and teaching

Use of Technology

Open universities use a variety of communication technology. A notable feature of open universities system is 'the planned use of wide range of media.... suited to the needs of the students.'

Lewis classifies the technologies used in distance education into three main groups, i.e. audio technologies, video technologies and computer based technologies. A further distinction is the mode of utilisation which can be either one way or two way.

Bates who has rich and varied experience in the use of technology in distance education and who has written extensively on the role of technology in open and distance learning suggested that distance teaching institutions' decision making on the use of technology should depend on the analysis of the following seven criteria:

- *Access*: How accessible is a particular technology for learners? How flexible is it for a particular target group?
- *Costs*: What is the cost structure of each technology? What is the unit cost per learner?
- *Teaching and Learning*: What kinds of learning are needed? What instructional approaches will best meet these needs? What are the best technologies for supporting this teaching and learning?
- *Interactivity and User-friendliness*: What kind of interaction does this technology enable? How easy is it to use?
- *Organizational issues*: What are the organizational requirements, and the barriers to be removed, before this technology can be use successfully? What changes in organization need to be made?
- *Novelty*: How new is this technology?
- *Speed*: How quickly can courses be mounted with this technology? How quickly can materials be changed.

Academic Programmes

The academic programmes offered by open universities reflect the underlying philosophies that brought them into existence. The following four considerations seemed to have been particularly important in the academic planning of open universities:

1. Demand for trained personnel
2. Human capital theory
3. Liberal arts tradition
4. Concern with lifelong learning

Academic programmes offered by open universities are differently categorized by different distance educators. A simple classification of distance courses is four fold (Anthony Kye, 1981):

- Academic courses
- Vocational courses
- Recreational courses
- Literacy and Numeracy courses

Smith, former Pro-Vice Chancellor of the UKOU, classified academic programmes into seven broad categories (Smith):

- Training courses
- Awareness courses

- Updating courses
- Academic courses
- Conversion courses
- Upgrading courses
- Language courses

Kulandai Swamy, former VC of IGNOU, categorized the courses offered by an open university under six heads:

- Programmes that have no comparable courses in conventional institutions (Non-conventional programmes).
- Programmes of specific job relevance/job-orientation (job oriented programmes).
- Programmes seeking to cater to the unfulfilled or newly developed aspirations which may not have any immediate job relevance to the learners (Programmes of Lifelong Education).
- Programmes of offer for wide options for those within conventional system (Open Programmes for Conventional Students).
- Programmes of specific social welfare orientation (Welfare Orientation Programmes).
- Programmes seeking to upgrade/update the skills and qualifications of professional and others with a focus on an immediate job oriented objective (Programmes of Continuing Education).

Open Universities' academic programmes generally meet the following criteria:

- useful to the market
- useful for social activities outside the labour market
- contribute to scientific and/or cultural education
- alternative for large number of students
- not exceed fixed cost
- appropriate for distance teaching
- alternate the teaching capacity problems of existing institutions
- useful to the people who wish to study the medical and engineering courses who may not get seats in conventional universities.

Course Development

Course development in open universities comprises course

planning and course production. Each open university follows its own method of course production. Normally one of the following six models is adopted.

- Content specialist model
- Content specialist and editor model
- Content specialist and transformer model
- Course specialist and transformer model
- Instructional design model
- Course team model

The last model has many special features. It was pioneered the British Open University and has since been adopted with modifications by several open universities.

Perry, the first Vice-Chancellor of the UKOU, claimed that the concept of the course team is the single most important contribution of the U.K. Open University to teaching practice and that a course produced by this method will inevitably tend to be superior in quality.

Instructional System

A distinguishing feature of open university system is its multi media instructional system. Multi-media instructional system is mostly learner based, while the instructional system in a conventional university is teacher based. In this system teachers are absent and learners are independent and mostly learn for themselves with the help of multi-media instructional packages. It is said that in a distance system the institution teaches whereas in a conventional system the teacher teaches.

Broadly, the instructional system of an open university consists of the following:

1. Print
2. Broadcast Audio-Visual
3. Non-Broadcast Audio-Visual
4. Practical/Project work
5. Inter-Personal Communication

Open universities use a variety of media. For example the British Open University's Charter specifically enjoins it to advance and disseminate learning and knowledge 'by teaching and research by a diversity of means such as broadcasting and technological devices appropriate to higher education'. One of the objectives of the Indria Gandhi National Open University is 'to advance and disseminate learning and knowledge by a diversity of means including the use of any communication technology..."

The components of instructional systems of the UKOU and IGNOU are given below:

Open University UK:

- Specially structured course books
- Radio and TV programmes
- Assignments marked by a Tutor (Tutor-marked Assignments TMAs) or by Computer (Computer Marked Assignments CMAs).
- Course end examination
- Residential schools
- Home experiment kits
- Computing

Indira Gandhi National Open University:

- Self-instructional printed materials
- Face to face counselling
- Lab practicals/training
- Audio and video cassettes
- Radio broadcasting
- TV broadcasting
- Internet based delivery
- Tele-counselling/Tele-conferencing
- Practical training.

Learner Support

Research and practice of distance teaching-learning proved that self instructional print and non-print materials are not fully supportive of distance learning, because they fail to solve several of problems faced by distance learners. Some of such problems faced by a distance student are:

- isolation from fellow students
- isolation from continuous pressure of teachers.
- lack of opportunity for comparisons of his performance with fellow students

- time gap between submission and receipt of assignment responses
- lack of appropriate reading and study skills
- lack of library facilities
- lack of enough time for study
- personal problems

These problems cannot be solved by learning packages provided to students. Hence they need additional support to overcome the problems. Increasingly distance teaching institutions are acknowledging that their students need support beyond what is provided by teaching staff and teaching materials. The quality, quantity and efficiency of student support services are significant in distance teaching institutions.

> Student support, in broader terms, is all the activities beyond the production and delivery of course materials that assist in the progress of students in their studies. According to Ormond Simpson (Simpson 2000), the Director of the U.K. Open University's Centre for Educational Guidance and Student Support, it falls into broad areas. The first is academic (or tutorial) support which deals with supporting students with the cognitive, intellectual and knowledge issues of specific courses or set of courses. This will include, for example, developing general learning skills, numeracy and literacy. The second is non-academic or counselling support which deals with supporting students in the affective and organizational aspects other studies. There are further sub divisions within these two divisions.

In a distance teaching university, student support services are built on the concept of local centres. Local centres are normally of two kinds—regional and study centres.

Staff Development

'Staff development' is the new term for 'training' in distance education literature. Staff development refers to "the acquisition of knowledge and skills that people who work in distance education system need."

Staff development is one of the priority activities of a distance teaching system. In most of the countries a large number of personnel in distance education institutions are drawn from the conventional education system and hence training becomes imperative for equipping them with necessary knowledge, skills and aptitudes to perform the new tasks in the new systems.

The need for training distance educators is well expressed by the UNESCO Regional Office for Education in Asia and Pacific in the following words. ".... The lack of trained personnel is a stumbling block. Most of the people, working in distance education have come from formal system and are attending to the methods of traditional education. Their new roles demand a new set of skills and attitudes, personnel must be reoriented and retrained for their changed task..."

There are several theoretical and practical objectives of staff development. The Commonwealth of Learning (COL) Round Table Conference on Training (1990), emphasizing the importance of adequately trained manpower to improve the quality of distance education stated that training programmes should:

- suit needs of the institution
- be available to all categories of staff
- suit the experience of the staff
- provide a sequence of training opportunities
- offer scope for career advancement
- employ a variety of strategies.

Most strategies used for staff development in the conventional systems of education are used for distance education systems also. The following are the popular strategies used for staff development:

- Workshops
- Field staff programmes
- Manuals
- Professional associations
- In-house programmes
- Assistance from resource institutions
- Consultancy
- Attachments
- Visits
- Adoptions

Analysis

Rumble and Keegan selected five general areas for analysis of open universities:

1. What are their objectives?
2. What kinds of students are attracted to OUs?
3. What media do the OUs use and to what extent they are making use of new educational media?
4. How good are their academic standards?
5. How cost-effective are they?

Rumble and Keegan found from their analysis the following common characteristics of open universities:

- A conscious and systematic approach to the design of learning materials for independent study.
- The use of a wide range of media and other resources to teach, necessitating a variety of production and distribution systems appropriate to the media in use.
- Associated with the use of the various media, a marked role differentiation of staff.
- The centralised design and production of materials, combined with localised learning.
- Marked division of labour between those responsible for materials design and production and those responsible for tuition and assessment.
- The provision of two way communication between students and tutors.
- The introduction into academic community of a number of quasi industrialised processes which require appropriate management techniques.

Factors in the Success

Perry, recalling his experiences as the founder Vice-Chancellor of the UKOU listed the following four most important and critical factors in the UKOU's success:

- The fighting spirit of the staff engendered by the widespread scepticism about its success in 1969.
- The determination, staying power and success rates o the students. The University was for many of them emancipation.
- The care, almost paternal in nature, that part-time tutors took over the well-being of their students both academic and otherwise.
- The fact that all teaching was open to view by public and by the academic world that could thus recognize the continued quality of the courses.

According to the founder Rector of the Fern University (Germany) following seven factors contributed to the success of the University:

1. Attractive to students
2. Acceptance by scholars
3. Institutional growth
4. Establishment of a new place for scientific research
5. Development of technology based system of teaching and learning
6. The emergence of new types of students
7. Favourable career prospects of graduates

Open universities have the power to alter traditional teaching and learning systems structurally and to accelerate change.

They point towards the future of an information and learning society in which its concepts and experience will be more important and relevant than they are today.

Profiles of Popular Open Universities

2

Allama Iqbal Open University, Pakistan

Allama Iqbal Open University (AIOU) is the first Open University in Asia. AIOU is a unique institution in Pakistan because of its philosophy, system, approach, functions and overall structure. The University with its main campus at Islamabad and huge network of regional centers spread all over the country is serving its clientele all over Pakistan and in the Middle East. AIOU is a distance education institution, which provides multi disciplinary education from basic to doctoral level programmes.

AIOU, when established in 1974, was the second Open University in the world and first in Asia and Africa. It, thus, speaks of the foresight of the policy-makers of that time. As these past years of AIOU have proved, distance education has opened up new opportunities for millions, particularly women, and supplemented the efforts of the federal and provincial governments in a big way and that too without becoming a burden on their resources.

Allama Iqbal Open University was established in May 1974 under Act No. XXXIX passed by the Parliament of Pakistan. It was initially named as the People's Open University, renamed as Allama Iqbal Open University in 1977 at the eve of the first centenary of the national poet and philosopher, Allama Muhammad Iqbal. The idea of an "open university" was presented with the enunciation of broad principles in the Education Policy of 1972-80, in these words:

> "Open universities are being used in several countries to provide education and training to people who cannot leave their homes and jobs for full time studies. An open university will, therefore, be established to provide part-time educational facilities through correspondence

courses, tutorials, seminars, workshops, laboratories, television and radio broadcasts and other mass communication media...."

The main objectives of the University as enunciated in the Act are as under:

- To provide educational facilities to people who cannot leave their homes and jobs in such manner as it may determine.
- To provide such facilities to the masses for their educational uplift as it may determine.
- To provide facilities for the training of teachers in such manner as it may determine.
- To provide for instruction in such branches of learning technology or vocations as it may deem fit, and to make provision for research and for the advancement and dissemination of knowledge in such manner as it may determine.
- To hold examinations and to award and confer degrees, diplomas, certificates and other academic distinctions.

Factors Influencing the Starting of Open University

In 1971, on the eve of launching an open university, participation rates at primary, middle, secondary and higher levels of education were 40 per cent, 20 per cent, 12 per cent and 2.5 per cent respectively. In spite of setting impressive targets for achieving higher participation rates, real achievements invariably remained low. The need for finding alternative means of providing educational opportunities was thus critical, particularly in rural areas where three quarters of the country's population lived. Additionally, equality of educational opportunity needed to be assured for deprived sections of society.

Pakistan had lagged behind its neighbours in the period up to the establishment of AIOU. The existing educational system was unable to meet the growing needs of a rapidly changing society. Thus, the justification for new additional educational system was felt.

Another reason for the new additional system of education was that socio-economic developments was only possible when education and training opportunities were made available to all and for all their lives. A comprehensive continuing education programme needed to be launched and made readily accessible to all who desired it.

Technological advances had contributed to the emergence of open distance learning. The application of ICT, thus, offered a solution to Pakistan's educational problems. Such an opportunity helped democritisation of education. The successful use of ICT by UKOU made its use in Pakistan possible.

The other major factor considered was the convenience of the learner. As stated by Holmberg (1986) the basic arguments in favour of distance education... are the opportunities opened to adults to learn anywhere and at any time suitable to them beside their other commitments to upgrade their competence and generally to educate themselves, without having to adopt themselves to the convenience of others.

The establishment of AIOU was a giant step towards the ultimate goal of providing equal educational opportunities for the people of the region and of developing open universities. It was a regional response to the developments that had followed from the establishment of UKOU and that provided so sound support for the development of AIOU itself.

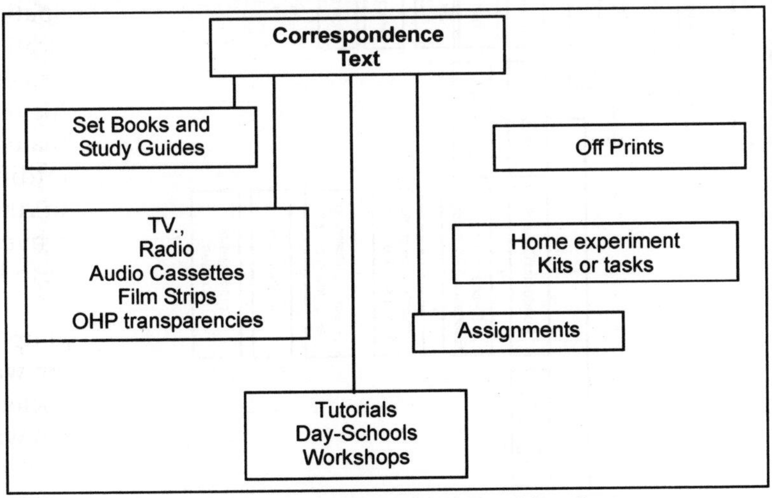

The Components of the AIOU Teaching System

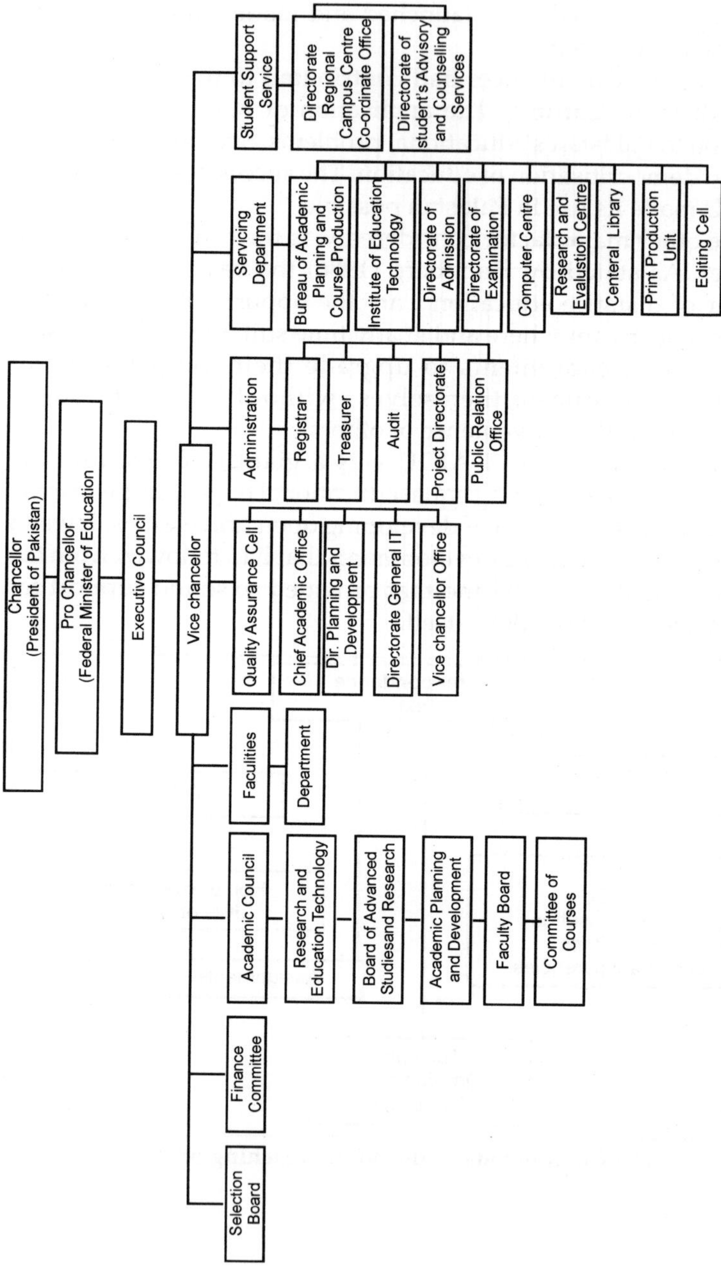

Administrative Structure (Allama Iqbal Open University)

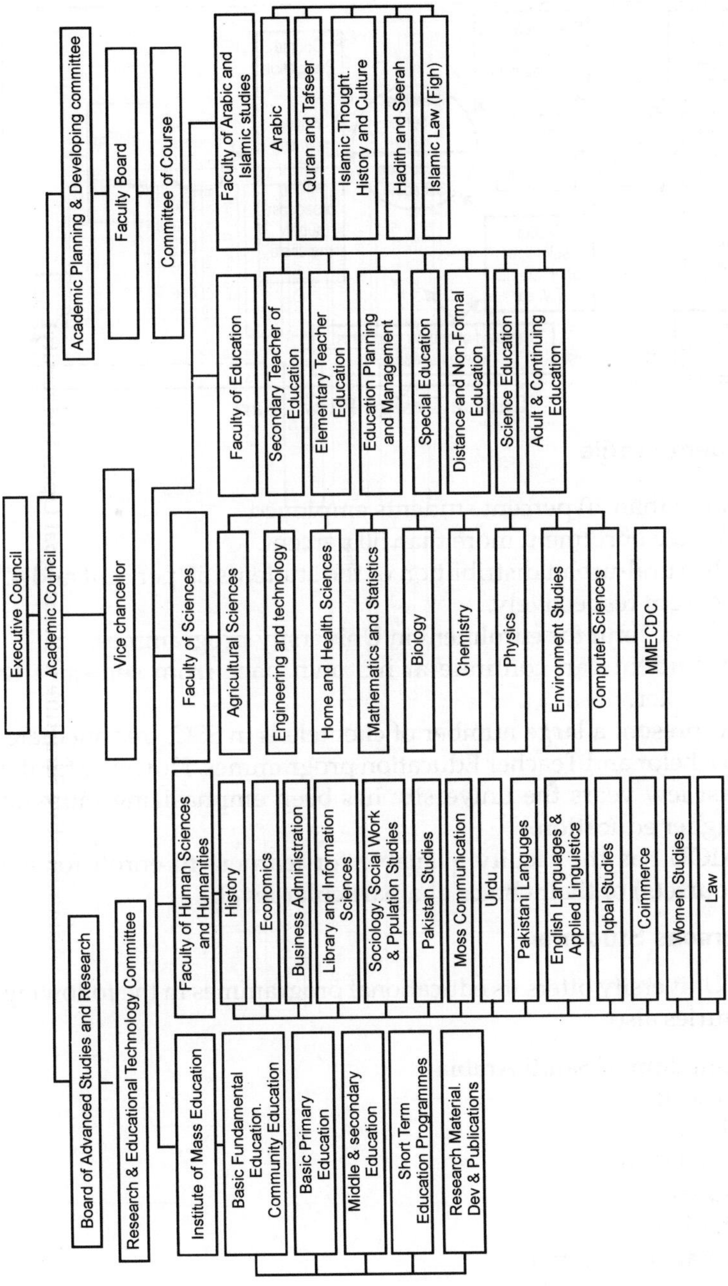

Academic Structure (Allama Iqbal Open University)

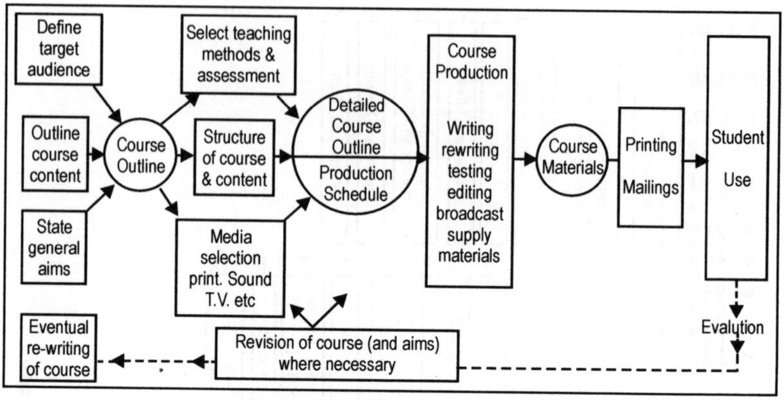

Course Design Flow Chart

Student Profile

- More than 70 percent students employed.
- Female enrolment more than 50 percent.
- The rural-urban distribution of the students 58 per cent and 42 per cent respectively.
- No age limit for enrolment in University programmes.
- A student can continue at his own pace from semester to semester.
- At present a large number of clientele is in SSC, Intermediate, Bachelor and Teacher Education programmes. However for the last few years the university has been emphasizing more on higher education.
- AIOU has the facility available for learners to enroll for the course(s) of their choice at a particular level.

Overseas Students

The University offers its educational programmes in the following countries also:

- Kingdom of Saudi Arabia
- Kuwait
- Qatar
- Abu Dhabi
- Dubai
- Sharjah
- Sultanate of Oman
- Bahrain

Faculties

Faculty of Arabic and Islamic Studies

Established in 1974, the Faculty has been upgraded as the Faculty of Arabic and Islamic Studies in 1998, with the following departments:

- Arabic Language and Literature
- Hadith and Seerah
- Islamic Law (Fiqh)
- Islamic Thought, History and Culture
- Quran and Tafseer

Faculty of Education

Established in 1984, the Faculty of Education's origin predates the university. A National Institute of Education was established in 1973 as a part of the Federal Ministry of Education, to improve education at school levels through in-service training of Master Trainers. This institute became a part of the University in June 1975. The Faculty of Education has the following departments:

- Adult and Continuing Education
- Distance and Non-Formal Education
- Educational Planning and Management
- Science Education
- Special Education
- Teacher Education (Secondary)
- Teacher Education (Elementary)

Faculty of Sciences

Renamed as Faculty of Sciences, the Faculty of Basic and Applied Sciences was established in 1982. It comprises the following nine departments:

- Agricultural Sciences
- Biology
- Chemistry
- Information Technology
- Computer Sciences
- Engineering and Technology
- Environmental Sciences
- Home and Health Sciences

- Mathematics and Statistics
- Physics

Faculty of Social Sciences and Humanities

The Faculty of Social Sciences and Humanities was established in 1982. The departments of the Faculty are:

- Business Administration
- Commerce
- Economics
- English Language and Applied Linguistics
- History
- Iqbal Studies
- Library and Information Sciences
- Mass Communication
- Pakistan Studies
- Pakistani Languages
- Sociology, Social Work and Population Studies
- Urdu
- Gender and Women's Studies

Instructional System

Allama Iqbal Open University, being a distance education institution, relies heavily on all varieties of available media to reach its students in an effective manner. The main components of its multi media package are the following:

- Correspondence materials including self-learning study package and supplementary study materials (readers, textbooks and study guides).
- Radio and television broadcasts generally relate to the study materials of the package.
- Satellite transmission: AIOU is putting on air its educational media material on PTV-2 which is beaming out its transmission through satellite to more than 45 countries.
- Online Teaching: Various regions have already been linked for online education and online classes through teleconferencing have been started for Computer Science programmes.
- Video Conferencing: Computer Science department has also successfully conducting a series of video conferencing lectures with US and other scholars in past semesters.

- Non-broadcast media including slides, audio cassettes, fillip charts, and leaflets (generally for basic functional and literacy level courses) and also audio/video cassettes is an integral part of learning material.
- Tutorial instruction through contact sessions and academic guidance facilities at study centres (mostly in the afternoons).
- Face-to-face teaching has recently been started for those courses, which require intensively practical/lab work or skill development.
- Group training workshops for post graduate programmes, generally at M.A/M.Sc/M.Phil and Diploma levels.
- Internship of short term and long term duration in industrial or business concerns for B.B.A. and M.B.A. programmes.
- Course assignments as an instrument of instruction, continuous assessment and general academic guidance of students. These assignments are evaluated by the respective tutors.
- Final examination is held for each course, at the end of the semester.

Academic Programmes on Offer

Academic Programmes: The university has introduced a wide range of undergraduate, graduate, Master's, M.Phil, and Doctoral Programmes. These programmes have given distinction to the University in relation to other educational institutions of Pakistan as it caters to the need of all age groups and levels of education. These programmes are enlisted below.

Ph.D Programmes: Based on M.Phil Degree 1. Iqbal Studies 2. Urdu 3. Islamic Studies 4. Distance and Non-Formal Education (DNFE) 5. Teacher Education (Secondary), 6. Educational Planning and Management (EPM), 7. Special Education, 8. Agricultural Extension 9. Statistics 10. Mathematics.

MS/M.Phil Leading to Ph.D: 1. Food and Nutrition 2. Distance and Non-Formal Education (DNFE), 3. Teacher Education (Secondary), 4. Educational Planning and Management (EPM), 5. Special Education, 6. Statistics, 7. Chemistry, 8. Islamic Studies 9. Pakistani Languages and Literature.

MS/M. Phil Programmes: 1. Islamic Studies 2. Iqbal Studies 3. Urdu 4. Teacher Education (Secondary), 5. Educational Planning and Management 6. Distance and Non-formal Education 7. Special

Education 8. Mass Communication 9. Statistics 10. Economics 11. Chemistry 12. Food and Nutrition 13. Pakistani Languages and Literature.

M.Sc. (Hons.): Year Education 1. Agriculture Extension (Regular classes at main campus, 2. Live Stock Management AIOU, Islamabad) 3. Rural Development (For continuing students only).

MA/MSc-Year Education: Master of Science (M.Sc.) 1. Pakistan Studies 2. Mass Communication 3. Economics 4. Community Health and Nutrition 5. Physics 6. Forestry Extension, 7. Environmental Design, 8. Sociology, 9. Mathematics 10. Chemistry, 11. Statistics 12. Gender and Women Studies.

Master of Arts (M.A.): 1. Teaching of English as a Foreign Language (TEFL), 2. History, 3. Islamic Studies, 4. Arabic, 5. Urdu, 6. Teacher Education, 7. Educational Planning and Management (EPM), 8. Distance and Non-Formal Education, 9. Special Education 10. Business Administration (MBA), 11. MBA (Banking and Finance) 12. MBA (Information Technology), 13. Commonwealth MBA (for Executives), 14. Commonwealth MPA (for Executives) 15. Library and Information Sciences (MLIS).

Other Programmes Offered by the University

M.Ed. Programme: 1. Teacher Education (Secondary), 2. Distance and Non-formal Education, 3. Special Education, 4. Science Education.

Postgraduate Diplomas: (PGD) 1. Teaching of English as a Foreign Language (TEFL) 2. Dietetics (For Dieticians) 3. Nutrition (For Physicians), 4. Women Studies, 5. Mass Communication, 6. Educational Planning and Management (EPM), 7. Computer Science (Online), 8. Commonwealth Executive Business Administration, 9. Commonwealth Executive Public Administration, 10. Environmental Design, 11. Youth in Development Work (only at Rawalpindi/Islamabad).

Teacher Education Programmes: 1. Bachelor of Education (B.Ed General), 2. Bachelor of Education (B.Ed Arabic), 3. Certificate of Teaching (CT), 4. Diploma in Education (10+3 Model), 5. Primary Teaching Certificate (PTC), 6. Arabic Teachers Training Course (ATTC).

Bachelor Degree Programmes: 1. B.A. (General) 2. B.Com. (Commerce) 3. B.B.A. (Business Administration) (Regular classes) 4. B.M.C. (Bachelor of Mass Communication) 5. B.L.S. (Bachelor of Library and Information Sciences) 6. B.A. (Dars-e-Nizami)

7. Bachelor of Engineering (Telecommunication) 8. Bachelor of Technology (Automobile) 9. Foundation Semester (BS-CS) (For below 45% marks at intermediate level) 10. Bachelor of Science (Computer Science) BS (CS) 11. B.Sc. in Vision Sciences.

Diplomas (Undergraduate): 1. Vision Sciences leading to B.Sc. 2. Computer Graphics.

Secondary School Certificate (SSC): 1. H.S.S.C (General) 2. H.S.S.C. (I.Com) 3. H.S.S.C. Dars-i-Nizami. 4. F.Sc. Family and Community Health 5. Home Economics 6. F.Sc. Pre-Medical 7. F.Sc. Pre-Engineering.

SSC (Matric): 1. S.S.C (General) 2. S.S.C (Dars-e-Nizami) 3. S.S.C (Health) 4. S.S.C. (Home Economics)

Certificate Level Courses: 1. Certificate in Librarianship 2. French Online 3. Selling of Home Made Products 4. Arabic Bol Chaal 5. Al-Lisan-ul-Arabi 6. Computer Graphics.

Another feature of the University's programmes is the provision of non-credit courses of six-month duration, which mainly of three type's i.e. 1. Functional Non-credit Courses 2. Technical Course 3. Agricultural Course.

Open Tech. Courses (Non-credit): The University has been offering over 43 courses in this programme. (For students of Rawalpindi and Islamabad only).

Short Term Educational Programmes (STEPS): The University has developed and launched about 90 STEPS courses in the following areas of studies: 1. Management Sciences (22 courses) 2. Social Sciences (15 courses) 3. Hotel Services (05 courses) 4. Community Education (17 courses) 5. Agricultural Courses (06 courses).

Course Development Process

Course development process at AIOU comprises the following steps (Rashid, 2000):

- Need assessment of target population.
- Preparation of schemes of studies
- Keeping the course outlines at par with other formal courses.
- Formulation of course teams.
- Meeting of committee of courses.
- Approval from faculty board.
- Getting approval from research and educational technology committee.

- Presentation of outlines in Academic Planning and Development Committee for approval.
- Final approval from Academic Council.
- Monitoring of Writers.
- Reviewing the material.
- Sending material to bureau of AP&CP.
- Coordination with the course editor, designer and illustrator.
- Forwarding material to print unit through AP&CP.
- Final proof reading of press copy.
- To O.K. for mailing after printing of material.

Pakistan *Journal* of Education

Pakistan Journal of Education (PJE) is a high quality open access peer reviewed research journal of Faculty of Education (FOE), Allama Iqbal Open University. The Journal is dedicated to publish researches in the field of education. The journal welcomes research studies, book reviews and papers on the advancements in teaching and learning process, pedagogy, psychosocial aspects of the learner, economical and social nature of education, utilization of educational technology and many more. It also includes research papers in the field of curriculum, teaching methodologies, educational planning and management, special education, science education, measurement and evaluation, vocational training and rehabilitation, inclusive education etc.,

The Journal is published twice a year under the umbrella of Faculty of Education. The Journal is published in dual modes: i.e., print as well as online. It provides opportunity for the academicians, practitioners, researchers, professionals and scholars to share the knowledge through high quality theoretical and empirical research papers and book reviews.

Research and Evaluation Centre

The Research and Evaluation Centre (Previously known as Research and Statistical Services) was established at the end of 1983. Before this independent entity however it functioned as a "Research Cell" located in the Institute of Education.

The main objectives of the Centre are to:

- Conduct institutional research on all aspects of the distance learning system of Allama Iqbal Open University;
- Collect statistical data and prepare a statistical profile of AIOU;

- Conduct academic research in collaboration with academic departments;
- Work as Clearing House for the dissemination of research findings and statistical data.

Accordingly, the Research Centre had to reformulate its activities to provide a comprehensive action plan, first by concentrating on the distance learning system and secondly the extent to which it could contribute to the advancement of the educational field as a whole.

Long Term Plans: The Centre devises ways and means to study and research on the working of the open learning system of the AIOU, keeping itself abreast with the knowledge and researches done or being done in similar institutions around the world. The major emphasis is to keep the open learning system fully alive national and international demands.

Short Term Plans: The areas of activity on a short-term basis are:

1. Institutional Research

1.1. Primary focus: determination of effectiveness, quality assurance and evaluation of all aspects of the AIOU System (both formative and summative. 1.2. Secondary focus: need assessment/determination, evaluation and advice to other institutions.

2. Statistics and Surveys 3. Academic Research Advice 4. Institutional Problems and Coordination.

Areas for Research

1. Institutional Research

1.1 Courses and their effectiveness 1.2 Tutorial support system 1.3 Assessment system 1.4 Student problems 1.5 Methods of course production 1.6 Cost effectiveness of courses 1.7 Out-come of courses and programmes 1.8 Servicing/Operational Departments 1.9 Administr-ation

2. Statistical Data Compilation and Survey

2.1 Gathering and publication of statistics on the AIOU system e.g. admissions, drop out, pass rate, student characteristics. 2.2 Pre-course surveys; post-course surveys. 2.3 Statistical surveys for other institutions. 2.4 Statistical advice and technical assistance (inter/external).

3. Academic Research Advice

Collaboration, advice and technical assistance to academic departments or individuals on specific research projects.

Compilation of various Statistical Supplements/queries, preparation of Introductory Brochure and Mini Prospectus of Educational Programmes of AIOU and Vice Chancellors' Annual Report etc. are the other regular/permanent activities of REC.

In late eighties, an evaluation mission sponsored by ODA and UKOU (Sargent, 1989) confirmed the successful operation of AIOU. The evaluation team concluded that AIOU had a continuing role to play in the future in a number of ways. There were specifically:

- Provision of lower level educational opportunities to people who had not completed their early schooling, particularly women, to enable them to produced to higher level opportunities.
- Provision of opportunities for higher education to people unable to attend conventional institutions.
- Provision of initial training for primary and secondary teachers.
- Provision of materials for updating and retraining of teachers.
- Testing and development of new educational approaches and resources.

3

Arab Open University, Kuwait

The idea of establishing a non-profit open university in the Arab world was initiated by the President of Arab Gulf Development Programme. In 1996 he officially announced the concept of establishing the Arab Open University as a non-conventional academic institution and as a foundation which contributes to steering development in scientific, social and cultural sphere. The initiative developed to a full pledged Arab Open University in 2002 in a strategic partnership with Open University in the United Kingdom.

The University occupies up in several Campuses located across the Middle East, including in Kuwait, Jordon and Lebanen. In 2003 Campuses were opened in Bahrain, Saudi Arabia, Egypt and Oman. The AOU is affiliated with the UK Open University.

Vision

A pioneering Arab Open University dedicated to building the science and knowledge society.

Mission

Develop and disseminate knowledge, and build experience according to international quality standards without time or geographical barriers for the sake of contributing and preparing manpower for development needs and to build science and knowledge society in the Arab countries.

AOU is seen as playing a key role in the development of human resources in all fields needed by the job market, as well as allowing the exposure to and use of modern technologies. AOU teaching and training programme is seen as a mechanism for upgrading the skills of the many thousands of students and teachers in the Arab World.

The headquarters are in Kuwait. Twenty two Arab countries eventually planned to be involved in the University.

AOU website explains its philosophy of "An Open System of Education", whereby it is flexible in its capacity to accommodate a "wider base of Higher Education Seekers".

Key Features

- Quality blended high education
- Upgrading teachers' skills
- Democratisation of education in Arab world
- Enabling Arab citizens, irrespective of background and circumstances, to gain access to higher education.
- Training students for the work place.

Undergraduate Programmes

The AOU offers three programmes co-awarded in collaboration with the United Kingdom Open University (UKOU). The AOU offering the following certifications:

IT Department

- B.Sc Computing
- B.Sc Computing with Business
- B.Sc Bachelor of Science in Information and Communication Technologies
- B.Sc Bachelor of Science in Information Technology and Computing

Business Department

- BA Business Studies-Accounting track

English Department

- BA English Language and Literature.
- BA English Language with Business.

Education Department

- BA Elementary Education
- BA Special Education-Mental Retardation

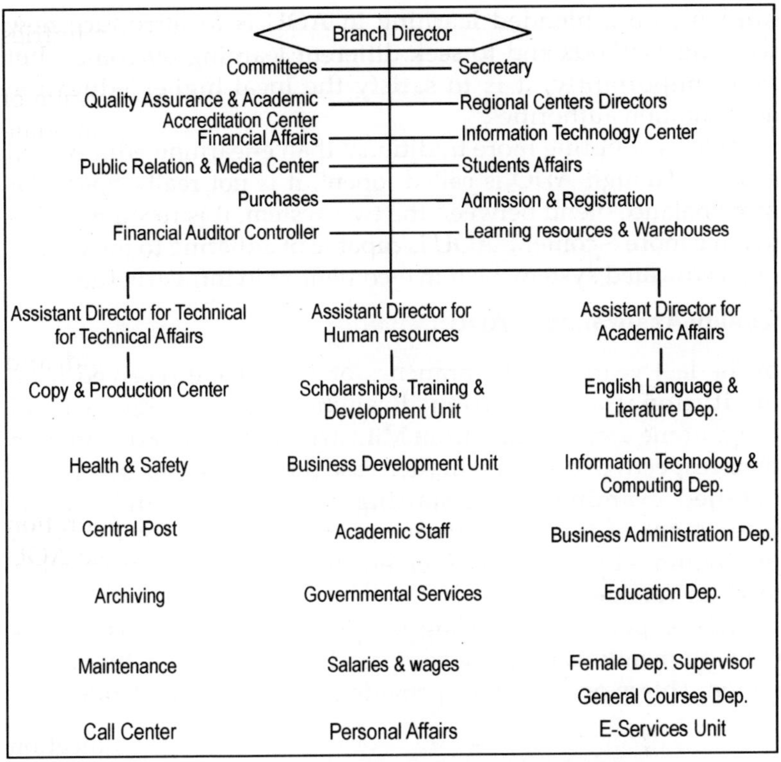

Arab Open University Organisational Chart

Evaluation of Blended Learning System

AOU has been implementing the blended learning system since 2002. AOU students' satisfaction with the blended learning was explored and found to be quite high. Blended learning essentially involves the application of e-learning techniques and tools along with face-to-face tutorials. The majority of faculty staff feels that their students access LMS on daily basis. They browse through the system for a multitude of activities. The curriculum packages in all the programme are very rich being affiliated with the UKOU.

The AOU has the privileges of using its state-of-the art curriculum. CDs come along with their package and are used by the students on individual basis.

Unlike other Universities where the move to blended learning is for financial and staffing reasons, the main reason behind implementing blended learning in AOU is to introduce new teaching methods and to seek different learning outcomes, but more importantly, it is to satisfy the local higher education accreditation authorities.

AOU is adopting more traditional than e-learning educational system. Though AUO is called 'open', it is not really open. For more balance blend between the two system, it is recommended to have more e-content. AOU is capable of adhering to the UKOU open educated system, be it in e-content or in infrastructure.

Quality Assurance in AOU

In the last years, all the branches of AOU have received local institutional accreditation. Branches have achieved local programme accreditation from Ministries of Higher Education in their respective countries. In each case the process has involved a detailed examination of staffing and facilities and critical assessment of the curriculum presented in each of the AOU programmes by a team of receivers drawn principals from other local universities.

AOU experience in setting its quality assurance system has made tremendous progress compared to other universities in the region. This experience may provide useful insight and guidance.

4

Athabasca University, Canada

Athabasca University is a world leader in online/and distance education. Students can study anywhere, any time and at their own place. Students from across Canada and 95 countries around the world could obtain a top quality postsecondary education without leaving their homes or workplaces.

Established in 1970, Athabasca University outgrew its Edmonton Campus by 1978 and moved north to its current location in Athabasca. The University has satellite locations in Calgary, Edmonton and St. Alberta.

The initial mandate was to offer undergraduate courses. Mandate was later revised to include graduate studies as well. In 1994, AU introduced the world's first online Executive MBA programme. Under the leadership of University President Dominique Abrioux. (1995-2005), AU expanded its programmes in all faculties.

Athabasca University's distinctive mission of improving accessibility, equality of opportunity and success of adult Canadians by removing barriers that traditionally restrict access to university level studies is fulfilled thorough a number of strategies described below:

- A commitment to an admission policy which dictates that the only entrance requirement to the University is that students be 18 years of age or older.
- A specialization in techniques of delivery and teaching that minimizes for students the constraints of time and place of study.
- A commitment to credit coordination allowing students to assemble credit earned at other institutions towards credentials at Athabasca University.

- A provision of special tutorial counselling and other support services that facilitate students' learning.
- The development of programmes in the light of identifiable needs of prospective students, including members of disadvantaged groups.
- A commitment to collaborative arrangements with other institutions with a view to improving the facilities and opportunities available to students.
- A commitment to continuous review of course content and delivery mechanism and their effectiveness.
- A commitment to identify elements of programme that may be better delivered and supported by the utilization of innovative pedagogy and appropriate education technologies.
- A commitment to the active search for adequate funding necessary for the realization of longer term objectives.

Athabasca University is engaged in a major strategy planning process relative to its mandate and mission.

Key Principles of AU's Distance Teaching

- Excellence
- Openness
- Flexibility
- Innovation

Academic Faculties and Centres

Effectively September 1, 2009, Athabasca University has changed its academic structure to better manage the institution's growth and diversity of course offerings. New faculties have been created, and the centers now fit within them.

Faculty of Business

- Undergraduate Courses and Programmes
- Masters Programmes
- Doctoral Programmes
- Leadership and Management development

Faculty of Health Disciplines

- Centre for Nursing and Health Studies
- Graduate Centre for Applied Psychology

Faculty of Humanities and Social Sciences

- Centre for Humanities
- Centre for Interdisciplinary Studies
- Centre for Social Sciences

Faculty of Science and Technology

- Centre for Science
- RAIC Centre for Architecture
- School of Computing and Information Systems

Faculty of Graduate Studies

- Graduate Programmes

Others Centers

- Centre for Distance Education
- Centre for Learning Accreditation (PLAR)
- Centre for Learning Design and Development
- Research Center
- Center for World Indigenous Knowledge and Research

Course Planning and Development

The University produces courses in three modules—the ground-up, the wrap around and the reading course modules. The ground-up comprises those courses that are written and produced in their totality by a course team. In wrap-around module, a course is developed with a suitable textbook as the core instructional material with the course team writing and producing elaborate workbook to guide the student through the text. The reading course module designed for senior level courses consists of assigned texts and are characterized by minimal guidance in the form of workbooks and increased tutorial supports.

The course design and development process encompasses various levels of linked activities, from long term planning to detailed course evaluation and revision. The phases are:

1. Long range institutional planning
2. Programme planning
3. Course design
4. Course development
5. Course materials production

Once the above 5 phases are completed, course deliverry in 6th phase and 7th phase is evaluation and its analysis.

Students

AU students come from every Canadian province and territory and 87 countries worldwide.

The average undergraduate is 29; the average graduate student is 39.

- 83 per cent work while they study.
- 67 per cent are women.
- 50 per cent graduate support dependents.
- 70 percent of graduate are the first in their family to earn a university degree.

Many students enrolled at other post-secondary institutions make extensive use of AU's courses and educational services to help them complete their degrees. These visiting students take AU courses for transfer to an academic programme at their home institution. Still others take AU courses out of personal interest or for professional development.

Delivery Methods

AU employs a board spectrum of distance learning methods and relies on a variety of information technologies to deliver course materials and instruction to students. These include the use of multi-media, online activities, print materials, web, e-mail, internet, CD-Rom, computer software, audio/video a combination of delivery methods. If a student registers for an online course, he will need access to a computer with an Internet connection.

Individualized Study

Most AU courses are also offered as individualized study courses. As a student in an individualized study course, one will receive learning resource package in the mail or online and work independently, with support and instruction from his tutor. He will work according to his own schedule, within the 6 (three-credit course) to 12 (six-credit course) month period allowed to complete the course

Grouped Study

Some AU courses are also offered as grouped study courses (a small number are available only through grouped study). As a student in a grouped study course, one would be one of a group of students simultaneously receiving instruction from an instructor, as he would in a conventional university setting. Grouped study courses are taught online or in classrooms at collaborating institutions across Canada and abroad and follow a traditional semester system, lasting 13 (three-credit course) or 26 (six-credit course) weeks.

Student Support

An AU student will benefit from an extensive network of student service including access to one-on-one support from faculty members, academic advisors, counselors, tutors, help-desk personnel and other support staff who will, together, provide a student with information, advice, and service.

A range of individualized accommodation and support service are available to students with physical, sensory, psychological or learning disabilities.

AU also offers nearly 200 scholarship, leadership awards and bursaries. Awards are available to both graduate and undergraduate students on the basis of academic achievement or financial need. All students are automatically considered for many of the academic scholarship; others are available by application. AU is also committed to facilitating student research and supports students in their research activities through an endowment for scholarships and funding for special research projects.

Benefits

Distance education through AU puts a student in control, allowing him to tailor his programme to his personal or professional needs and interest and to continue education without sacrificing personal, family, career or community commitments. Four aspects of distance education make it a particularly attractive option for busy people:

Accessibility

Whenever students, even if they are hundreds of miles from the nearest town, for them AU university campus is right there. AU students have completed courses and degrees while travelling abroad, while stationed in remote arctic outposts, while serving overseas with the Canadian Forces or with humanitarian groups and while completing as professional or Olympic athletes.

Flexibility

Students can take classes when it's convenient for them, at any time. AU's year-round admission and course registration policy allow students to enrole in a programme or start a course at any time of the year. They need not to wait until the beginning of a term or semester.

Affordability

AU course fees include the cost of printed or eText book and most other learning materials, and student can pay as they go: one course at a time, or more-whatever is best for them. Most importantly, undertaking distance study at AU does not require students to leave their jobs, home. The greatest cost associated with getting a degree from a conventional university lies not in the cost of the education itself but in lost income from taking time off work and the expense of living away from home for several years. More than 80 percent of AU students continue to work while they study.

Adaptability

One can complete an AU university certificate or diploma, a three-or-four-year bachelor's degree, a, master's degree or a doctorate; one can take one or more AU courses to transfer to one's programme at another post-secondary institution; or one can take one or more courses to just to satisfy his own interests or curiosity or for personal or professional development. Whatever be educational goal, one can achieve it at AU.

Student Support System

For the majority of the adult learners the concept distance learning is a new experience and lack the ability to adopt readily to such a system. In most cases, adult learner study part-time and have to accommodate their studies within the demands of their families, jobs and social life. Their role as a student is one of the many other roles. Further, most adult students have been away from educational environment for at least a few years so that their study habits are rusty.

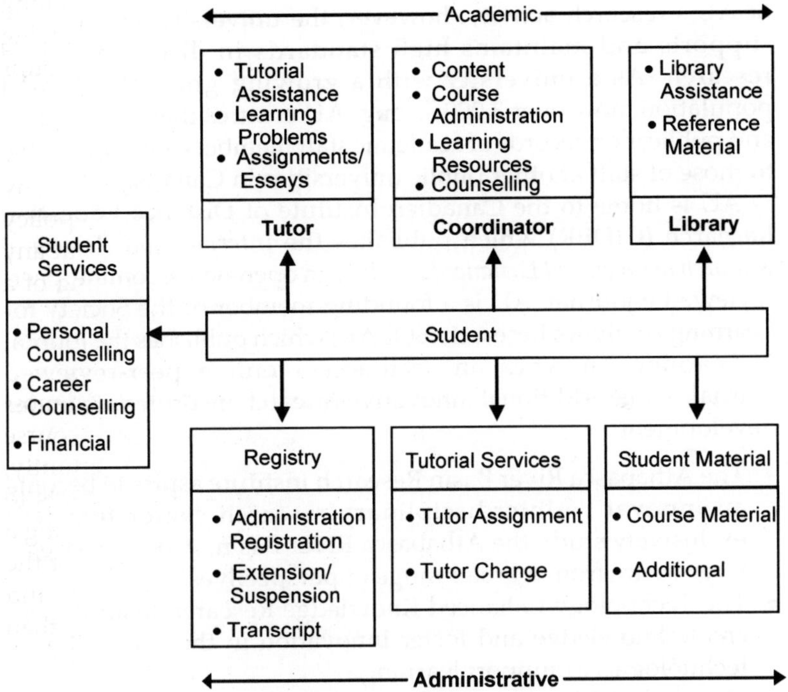

Student Support System

This creates conflict between the demands of their studies and those in other areas of their live. Students support services are provided by the University to minimize this conflict and help the students to proceed with the academic work in a systematic way to achieve success. Students support services are provide mainly by tutors and counselors.

Research

AU is committed to excellence in research and scholarship. Through the discovery, dissemination and transfer of new knowledge and the engagement of students at both the undergraduate and graduate levels, the university integrates research with creative teaching, thereby informing the curriculum and providing opportunities for highly qualified graduates to promote innovation and to participate more fully in society.

Mission critical research in the scholarship of teaching and learning in open and distance environments is the primary focus of AU's research activity; however, the university also actively supports and maintains high standards in discipline-based research. As a university with a growing graduate student population, now over 3,000 strong, AU ensures that the research and publication records of academic staff members are comparable to those of staff at other public universities in Canada.

AU is home to the Canadian Institute of Distance Education Research (CIDER) which publishes the *International Review of Research in Open and Distance Learning*, an open-access, online, peer-reviewed e-journal. AU is a founding member of the Society for Learning Analytics Research (SOLAR) which publishes the Journal of Learning Analytics, an open access, online, peer-reviewed journal. Three additional innovative research institutes are under development:

- The Athabasca River Basin Research Institute aspire to become an innovative interdisciplinary research center that will exclusively study the Athabasca River Basin, Alberta's largest river basin, from a broad range of perspectives.
- The Technology Enhanced Knowledge Research Institute will create knowledge and foster innovation in the use of digital technologies to support learning
- The Project Management Research Institute will initiate and strengthen cutting-edge, multi-disciplinary research in project management, enabling project management scholars, organization and practitioners to work together to address the significant challenges confronting project managers and project organizations.

5

Bangladesh Open University, Bangladesh

Bangladesh is a country of high absolute levels of poverty, the low per capita annual income $389, the high population growth, the low adult literacy rate, and the inability of the conventional education system to meet the country's requirements, including inadequate access in rural areas, inadequate higher and professional education and training opportunities, and the lack of informal and non-formal educational opportunities.

Bangladesh Open University, the only distance learning university in Bangladesh, was established on October 21, 1992 by an Act of Parliament to overcome the above difficulties. Its prime objective is to transform the country's vast human resources into an educated and trained work force by extending to them a wide range of academic programmes both formal and non-formal by using different delivery technologies.

The establishment was preceded by services of studies undertaken by the United Kingdom's Overseas Development Agency (ODA) between 1987 and 1989, and by the Asian Development Bank (ADB) between 1989 and 1991.

The rationale for the BOU project, spelt out in the ADB's Project Appraisal Document (ADB, 1992), cited

- the high absolute level of poverty,
- the low per capita GNP,
- the low adult literacy rate,
- the inability of the conventional education system to met the country's requirements,
- the inadequate higher and professional education and training opportunities,
- the poor quality of educational resources and programmes, and
- the lack of informal and non-formal educational opportunities.

The establishment of a distance teaching university would, it was believed, help support the government of Bangladesh's efforts to strengthen human resource development by increasing access to education and training in rural areas, provide higher education and professional training in selected areas, strengthening informal and non-formal educational programmes aimed at the general population, and enhance the general quality and relevance of educational programmes (ADB 1992).

Bangladesh had already gained some experience of distance education methods through the activities of the Bangladesh Institute of Distance Education (BIDE), set up to offer a Bachelor of Education degree to teachers, but there was little possibility of traditional universities taking the role of teaching external students by distance made. The only realistic option was to set up a new university to exploit distance teaching methods. Under the BOU Act, BIDE became a part of the new university.

Distance learning programmes of BOU are popular and are becoming popular in recent years because it can provide adults and/or female single parents with a second chance at a college education; reach those disadvantaged by limited time, money, distance or physical disability; update the knowledge base of workers at their places of employment; expand cultural background; learn a new language or start a degree programme that was postponed due to family or career needs.

Technology explosion in the field of distance education during recent years has not only revolutionized the teaching and learning environment but has also opened many new options for delivering distance education programme. A variety of technologies such as print, audio, video, audio graphics, audio conferencing, video conferencing, web conferencing and WWW are used for delivering distance-learning materials. BOU uses different delivery technology to extend education to every community, even to the most remote rural areas, thereby contributing to the alleviation of poverty. Age, time, place and pace do not restrict learners at BOU. Currently BOU has more than 300,000 students.

Academic Programmes

From the beginning, BOU was required to be more than a traditional university. The 1991 Feasibility Study indicated the nature of educational programmes to be offered by the University.

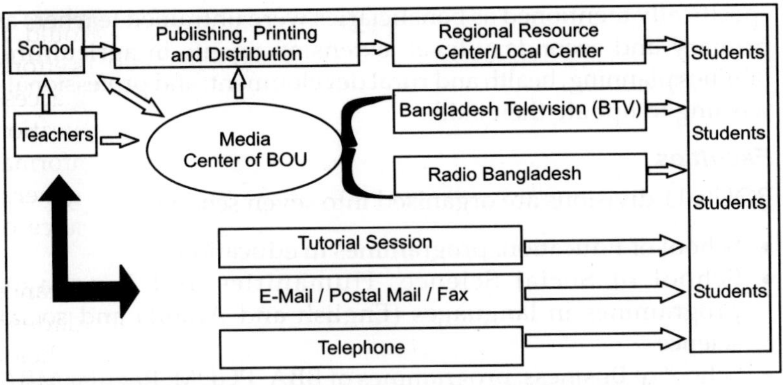

Operation of Bangladesh Open University

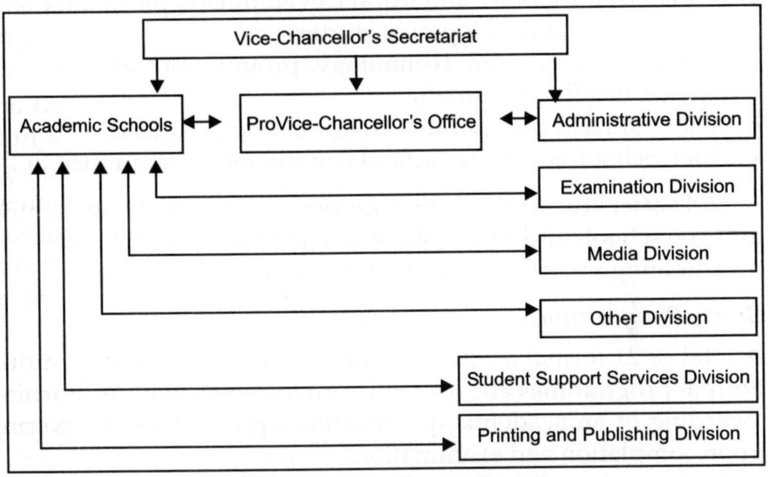

The Organizational Chart

The needs assessment survey demonstrated that there was a great demand for many of the programmes BOU proposed to offer.

BOU started serving those sectors of the population who were excluded from the traditional education system and those who, for one reason or other, had dropped out of traditional education. Particularly targeted were students is rural areas, and especially women, out of school youth, adults who had to work to support their families, and people in work who needed retraining, professional upgrading and personal development. Also specifically mentioned as beneficiaries were untrained teachers at primary and secondary level, extension agents in agriculture, families planning, health and rural development; and professionals wishing to update their skills.

Faculties

BOU's 11 divisions are organised into seven schools:

- School of Education: programmes in education
- School of Social Science, Humanities and Language: programmes in languages (English and Arabic) and social science
- School of Business: programmes of BBA, PGDM, Regular MBA and Commonwealth Executive MBA/MPA
- School of Agriculture and Rural Development: programmes in agriculture and development studies
- School of Science and Technology: programmes in computer science, health and nursing
- School of Law: programmes in law and legal studies
- Open School: secondary school completion programmes

BOU offers two types of programmes, formal and non-formal, in seven schools and a network of 12 regional resource Centres, 80 coordinating offices and 1,000 tutorial centres nationwide.

Study Programmes

A total of 21 formal academic programmes are offered by BOU. Formal programmes are academic programmes that result in the awarding of an academic qualification up to a Master's degree upon completion and examination.

As low rate of literacy remains an issue in Bangladesh, non-formal programmes are conducted by the BOU to create awareness and impart knowledge about health, environment, disaster management, basic science, agriculture, food, nutrition and other branches of knowledge for human development. To date, 19 non-formal programmes have been initiated in the areas of Environmental Protection, Basic Science, Elementary Mathematics, Agriculture, Bank Services, Marketing Management, Health, Nutrition, Population and Gender Issues.

Schools and Courses

School of Education

One of the oldest school of the university offering three formal programmes (MEd/BEd/CEd).

- Bachelor of Education (BEd)
- Master of Education (MEd)
- Certificate in Education (CEd)

School of Agriculture and Rural Development

School of Agriculture and Rural Development offering four formal programmes (B.Ag.Ed/DYDW/CLP/CPFP).

- Bachelor of Agricultural Education (B.Ag.Ed)
- Diploma in Youth Development Work (DYDW)
- Certificate in Livestock and Poultry (CLP)
- Certificate in Pisciculture and Fish Processing (CPFP)

School of Science and Technology

School of Science and Technology offering three formal programmes (B.Sc.-in-Nursing/DCSA/CS).

- B.Sc. in-Nursing (BSN)
- Diploma in Computer Science and Application (DCSA)
- B.Sc.in Computer Science

School of Social Science Humanities and Languages

School of Social Science Humanities and Languages offering four formal programmes (BA/BSS)/BELT/CALP/CELP).

- Bachelor of Arts (BA)/Bachelor of Social Science (BSS)
- Bachelor of English Language Teaching (BELT)
- Certificate in Arabic Language Proficiency (CALP)
- Certificate in English Language Proficiency (CELP)

Open School

Open School of the university offering two formal programmes (SSC/HSC)

- Secondary School Certificate (SSC)
- Highr Secondary School Certificate (HSC)
- Bachelor of Business Studies (BBS)

School of Business

School of Business of the university offering three formal programmes BBA/MBA/(CEMBA/CEMPA).

- Master of Business Administration (MBA)
- Common wealth Executive Master of Business Administration (CEMBA/CEMPA)
- Bachelor of Business Administration (BBA)

Delivery Technologies

Delivery Technologies are used to unite teacher and learners in distance education systems. Bangladesh Open University (BOU) mostly depends on Corresponding Model-print media as the basic delivery media in its programmes. It also uses multimedia model-the second generation of distance education (Taylor, 1995) such as audio-video technology. It also uses Tele learning model such as broadcast TV/Radio. Email and WWW are gaining increasing importance. But efforts are underway to introduce video conferencing and www-based materials for distance delivery. BOU are now supplying audio video materials (e.g. tapes, audio, and video) as a supplementary component of most of the programmes. Broadcasting (TV and Radio program) has been used to supplement the print material. Email is widely used for communication, enquiry, discussion, sending solved problems etc. There is no use of fourth generation and fifth generation models for distance education delivery at BOU right now.

The uses of non-print delivery technology for distance education in 2002 was significantly low compared to those of the previous years (1998 and 2000). Figure 2 illustrates the changes in actual use of non-print media from 1998 to 2002. In 1998, of the total 136 courses offered, 10 courses contained an audiocassette (7.4%). This percentage increased gradually to 8.3 per cent (17 courses out of the total 205 course) in 2000 and then it again slowly increased to 8.7 per cent in 2002.

There was only 3 per cent use of videotapes in 1998. This percentage increased to 5 per cent in 2000 (10 courses out of the total 205 course) and after that it slightly decreased to 4.3 per cent (10 courses out of the total 230) in 2002. Radio programme was used in 60 courses in 1998 (44%), which sharply decreased to 35 per cent (72 courses out of the total 205 course) in 2000 and then it has declined to 33 per cent in 2002.

The use of TV programme was 41 per cent in 1998. This percentage decreased to 34 per cent in 2000 after that it slightly increased to 35.2 per cent in 2002. There was no use of E-mail, CAL and Teleconference until 2000. The use of email was 5.4 per cent in 2000 after that it increased to 7 per cent in 2002. The use of CML/CAL (6.3%) started from 2000 and after that it increased to 9.6 per cent in 2002. In 2000, the use of teleconference was 2.4 per cent but it 2002 it decreased to 2.1 per cent. The trend of using computer aided learning, computer managed learning, email list are increasing till now. BOU is trying to adopt online technology and web based learning for its delivery.

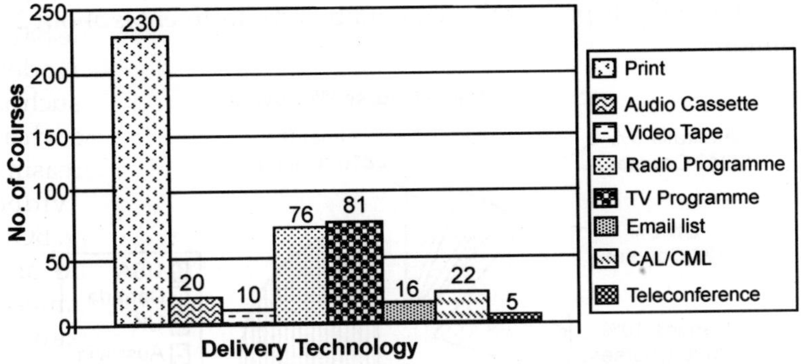

Fig. 5.1: The Use of different delivery technologies in 2002

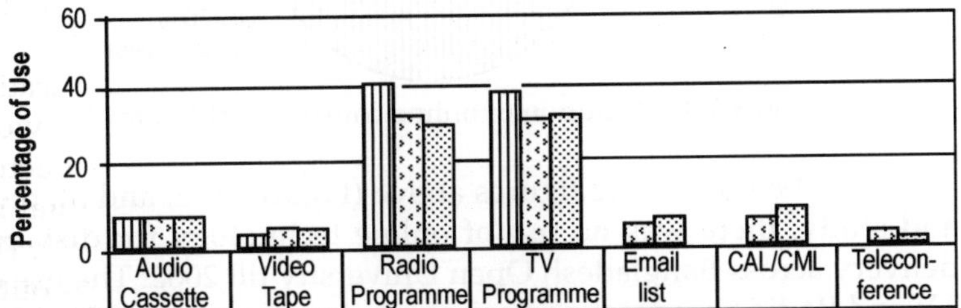

	Audio Cassette	Video Tape	Radio Programme	TV Programme	Email list	CAL/CML	Telecon-ference
1998	7.4	3	44	41	0	0	0
2000	8.3	5	35	34	50.4	6.3	2.4
2002	8.7	4.3	33	35.2	7	9.6	2.1

1998 2000 2002

Delivery Technoogy

Fig. 5.2: Comparison of different non-print media used in three different years

As Bangladesh is a developing country, Bangladesh Open University has not yet used any on-line technologies as a delivery technology. Bangladesh Open University is far more away from developed countries. Let's see some statistics. 89 per cent of online courses originate from North America. The USA is the first in offering with 70 per cent of all online courses worldwide. Canada is the second with 19 per cent of online courses. Australia, a country with a relatively small population is third with 3 per cent of online courses. But Bangladesh Open University (current enrolment: 300,000) can be regarded as Mega University. Mega Universities are large open Universities, each of which enrolled more than

100,000 students per year and its combined enrolment is about 2.8 million.

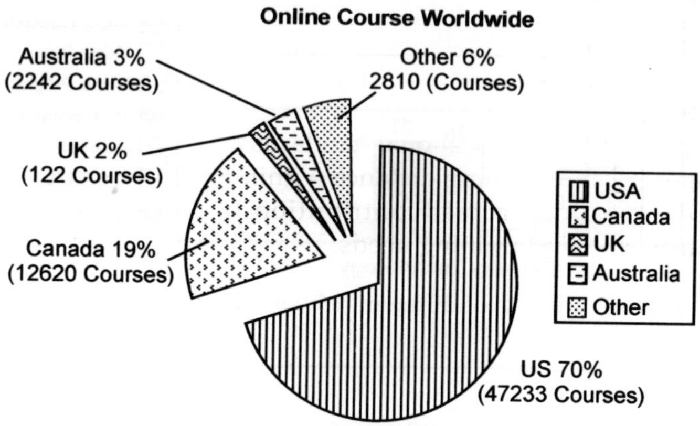

Fig. 5.3: Distribution of online courses worldwide

As can be seen in the figures above (Figures 1, 2, and 3), data and study, there was no use of online technology for distance delivery across Bangladesh Open University till 2002. The use of TV and Radio broadcasting has been decreasing until 2000. After that the use of radio programme has been decreasing while the use of TV programme has been increasing till 2002. But when considered as a percentage of the total number courses, the use of TV and Radio programme has been increased in 2002. There is an increasing trend of using CAL/CML and Email list at BOU till 2002. The following recommendations are given to increase the use of delivery technologies in Bangladesh Open University:

- Emphasize should be given on online Course delivery technology
- The extent of participation rates in each course that utilizes particular technologies should be investigated.
- WWW, Online course component should be included in every course at BOU

To what extent BOU fulfilled its mission? As stated by Rumble (1999) it

- met a wide range of indentified educational needs, both formal and non-formal.

- assisted the national development
- reached the many unreachable.
- helped democratisation of education to a considerable extent
- reached masses through the use of technology
- proved more cost-efficient and cost effective than traditional education system
- helped in raising educational standards through the high quality materials and teaching distance within Bangladesh.
- BOU is making a real contribution to meet the country's educational and training needs.

6

Fern Universitat, Germany

The **University of Hagen** (German: Fern Universitat in Hagen, informally often referred to as **FU Hagen**) is a public research university that is primarily focused on distance teaching. While its main campus is located in Hegen, North Rhine-Westphalia, Germany, the university maintains more than 50 study and research centers in Germany and throughout Europe. According to the Federal Statistical Office of Germany it is Germany's largest university.

The university was founded in 1974 as a public research university by the state Nodrhein-Westfalen and began its research and teaching activities in 1975. It was founded following the idea of UK's Open University to provide higher and continuing education opportunities through a distance education system in Germany.

The university awards the same qualifications as other Germany on-campus universities and maintains the same high requirements. Initially, the university had only three faculties with 1,304 full and part time students, but today the university has develop into Germany's leading intuition for distance education and is the only full university in that field with a student body of 83,536 students in the summer term of 2013 and 86,889 students in the winter term 2013/2014. Beside the substantial number of off-campus students, a considerable number of full-time postgraduate research students as well as more than 1,800 members of academic and research staff are based on the University of Hagen's main campus in Hegen.

The faculties of the University of Hegen award undergraduate, graduate and postdoctoral degrees (bachelor's, master's, doctorate degrees (Ph.Ds) and enable habilitation). All the degrees awarded by the University of Hegen are equivalent to those awarded by traditional Germany universities and up hold rigorous academic standards. The University of Hegen is awarding degrees and is doing research in the fields of Business Administration and Economics, Mathematics, Computer Science, Law, Psychology, Cultural Sciences and Political Science.

Organization and Administration

The Rectorate is the 'executive body' of the university, headed by Rector Helmut Hoyer. The Rectorate consist of the chancellor, Regina Zdebel, who is the head of the central administration and responsible for the university's budgeting, and three pro-rectors, who are responsible for international relations, teaching and communication, and research and structure respectively.

The Senate is the 'legislative branch' of the university. The rector and the member of the rectorate are senators ex officio, as are also the deans of the faculties, and the university's equal opportunities officer. Another 20 senators are elected for four-year terms, within the following quotas: eight university professors; four academic staff; four delegates of the student body; and four employees of the university administration.

The university council is the advisory board to the aforementioned entities and encompasses, among others, the former President of Germany Johannes Rau, as well as CEOs of German industries.

Faculties

After a 2006 structural reformation, the university consists of 4 faculties, which in turn comprise several disciplines, departments, and institute. As a consequences of the Bologna process, most faculties now offer Bachelor's, Master's, and Ph.D. degrees to comply with the new European degree standard. A notable exception is the undergraduate programme in law, from which students still graduate with the Staatsexamen (state examination), a central examination at Master's level held by the State of North Rhine-Westphalia. Each of the faculties is headed by a dean and a faculty council overseeing the research and teaching conducts.

The university is organized in four faculties:

- Faculty of Cultural and Social Sciences
- Faculty of Mathematics and Computer Science
- Faculty of Business Administration and Economics
- Faculty of Law

Study Material and Media

Teaching matter is not presented in an overcrowded lecture theatre, but in the form of well organized and prepared teaching materials, including study units, exercises, interactive CD-ROMs and DVDs which are delivered to the student's homes by mail, and increasingly via the Internet. Students can download additional material or listen to and watch online-lectures. They also hand in their assignments online.

Students Support

The characteristics of the Hagen distance education system alse include individual support, either at Hagen itself or through tutors at the study centres in Germany, Australia, Switzerland and Central and Eastern Europe. More recently, support is increasingly provided via the Internet: in chatrooms, for example, students discuss material-related questions and problem with the tutors. Thus, the FernUniversitat is able to meet students' needs for flexibility like probably no other university.

Study Programmes

Undergraduate Programmes

- Bachelor (B.Sc.) of Business Administration and Economics.
- Bachelor (B.Sc.) of Computer Science
- Bachelor (B.Sc.) in Cultural Studies
- Bachelor (B.Sc.) of Information Systems
- Bachelor (B.Sc.) of Laws
- Bachelor (B.Sc.) of Mathematics
- Bachelor (B.Sc.) of Pedagogy
- Bachelor (B.Sc.) of Political Science
- Bachelor (B.Sc.) of Psychology

Graduate Programmes

- Master (M.Sc) of Applied Computer Science
- Master (M.Sc) of Computer Science
- Master (M.Sc) in Management
- Master (M.Sc) of Economics
- Master (M.Sc) of Philosophy
- Master (M.Sc) of Laws
- Master (M.Sc) in Governance
- Master (M.Sc) of Psychology

The University of Hagen provides the opportunity to study for a Ph.D. on a part-time as distance option, or a full-time on-Campus basis in all of its disciplines offered.

Students (Winter Semester) 2014-15

Students (including students on sabbatical leave)-total		76,122
	Of whom men	53%
	Of whom women	47%
Students (without students on sabbatical leave)-total		75,080
Of whom	Regular students	68,089
	Academic students	4,168
	Students in further education programmes	2,823
Enrolled in the		
	Faculty of humanities and social sciences	41%
	Faculty of mathematics and computer science	14%
	Faculty of economics	34%
	Faculty of law	11%

Organization of Courses

The academic year is divided into two semesters. The winter semester runs from October 1-March 31 and the summer semester from April 1-September 30. Online and self-study courses are held from mid-October to mid-February and mid-April to mid-July. Additionally, the University of Hagen offers presence classes and special seminars, some of which are required to graduate successfully. Students can generally begin their studies in the winter or in the summer semester. The standard time required to finish a Bachelor's degree's course load 180 ECTS in full-time study is set at six semesters. The overall period of study for an undergraduate degree is divided into two parts: a period of basic study, equaling a course load of four semesters, at the end of which students must sit a formal examination, and a period of advanced study, equaling the course load of two semesters, after which students take their final examinations. Master's degrees, if done as full-time study, usually equaling the course load of four semesters. However, since a large proportion of the student body at the University of Hagen is studying in part-time, the regular study time can deviate but is not allowed to exceed a specific number of semesters.

Campus and Study Centers

Initially, FernUniversitat's departments were housed in rented apartments and buildings located all over Hagen and even outside the city. The development of Fern Universitat's campus near the roadways A 45 and A46 began in 1980 with the first office building Allgemeines Verfugungszentrum (AVZ I). Since the first building constructed several further buildings followed and increased the university campus, among them: The Eugen-Schmalenbach-Building (AVZII), the Philipp-Reis-Building, the Centre of Technology and Innovation (TGZ), the extension of the University Library, and the new canteen. As more and more university buildings are concentrated on the Campus, it has become easier for the academic staff of different academic areas to cooperate and engage in cross-disciplinary research.

Furthermore, as a distance university, the University of Hagen operates numerous regional and study centers located across Germany and in other European countries, which are an important aspect of the university's blended learning concept. At these regional and study centers students attend mandatory seminars and preparatory classes for exams, study together with other students, borrow books, and find mentors. Today, the university has more than 50 study centers within Germany and cooperates intensively with several other renowned institutions, such as Karlsruhe Institute of Technology, Goethe University Frankfurt, Johannes Kepler University of Linz or the University of Jena to broaden their teaching options and research.

Since the 1980s the University of Hagen has operated study centers on a joint basis with partner institutions abroad-first in the German-speaking countries and later also in the countries of Central and Eastern Europe. These study centers aim to spread information about the German language-based programmes of study offered via modern distance education, and they are intended to support students of the university. Furthermore, the faculties of the FernUniversitat and their international partner institutions of higher education jointly offer programmes of study leading to international dual degrees. The FU Hagen participates in the EU funding programmes in higher education and research.

Research

The University of Hagen supports focus-and profile-oriented research. Inerdisciplinary and cross-faculty collaboration leads to the grouping together of competencies and to the formation of competitive research focal points. At the same time, basic and applied research is the basis for promoting the new generation of academics.

Research Institutes

- *FIRM*—Forschungsinstitut fur rechtliches Informations management (Research Institute for Legal Information management)
- *FTB*—Forschungsinstitut Technologic und Behinderung (Research Center for Technology and Disabilities)
- *FTK*—Forschungsinstitut fur Telekommunikation (Research Institute for Telecommunication)
- *HIMS*—Hagener institute fur Managementstudien e.V. (Hagener Institute for Management Studies)
- *IKS*—instutut fur Kooperative System (Institute for Cooperative System)
- *IWW*—Instutut fur Wirtschaftswissenschaftliche Forschung und Weiterbilding GmbH (Institute for Economic Research and Training)
- *TestDaF-Institut* (Institute for Market Research)

Partnerships and Cooperations

In the fields of research and development the FU Hagens's faculties and chairs hold a wide array of diverse cooperations with renowned international scientific institutions, companies, associations (like the Kurt Haertel Institute for Intellectual Property) as well as public institutions. Furthermore, exchange of technology and knowledge is conducted through a variety of cooperation projects between science and industry, ranging from final theses by arrangement with the individual employer to commissioned research. Moreover, joint development of academic further education programmes with companies, associations and scientific institutions contributes to the interlinking of academia and practice.

The FU Hagen' faculties and institutions cooperate closely with numerous institutions of higher education (both traditional and distance teaching universities) and scientific institutions all over the world. The international cooperation agreements comprise all areas of the university: teaching, studies, research, administration and system development.

Success of University

Of the factors that contribute to the success of the Fern Unversitat, Otto Peter, its founder Vice Chancellor indicated seven factors:

- Attractivement of students
- Acceptance by scholars
- International growth
- Establishment of a new place for scientific research
- Development of technology based system of teaching and learning
- Emergence of new type of students
- Favourable career prospects of graduates

7

Indira Gandhi National Open University, India

Indira Gandhi National Open University, known as IGNOU, is a distance learning national university located in New Delhi, India. Named after former Prime Minister of India Indira Gandhi, the university was established in 1985, when the Parliament of India passed the Indira Gandhi National Open University Act, 1985. IGNOU is run by the central government of India.

IGNOU, the largest university in the world with over 4 million students, was founded to impart education by means of distance and open education, provide higher education opportunities particularly to the disadvantaged segments of society, encourage, coordinate and set standards for distance and open education in India and strengthen the human resources of India through education. Apart from teaching and research, extension and training form the mainstay of its academic activities. It also acts as a national resource center, and serves to promote and maintain standards of distance education in India.

History

In 1970 the Ministry of Education and Social Welfare in collaboration with the Ministry of Information and Broadcasting, the UGC and the Indian National Commission for Cooperation with UNESCO, organised a seminar on 'open university'. The seminar recommended the eastablishment of an open university in India on an experimental basis. The Government of India appointed an eight-member working group on open university in 1974. The leading role was given to G. Parthasarathi, the then Vice-Chancellor of the Jawaharlal Nehru University

The working group recommended establishing an open university by an act of Parliament as early as possible. University should have jurisdiction over the entire country so that, when it is fully developed, any student even in the remotest corner of the country can have access to its instruction and degress.

The working group suggested several measured to be followed in instructional and management processes of the open university which include: admission procedure, age releaxation, preparation of reading materials, setting up of core group scholars in different fields, setting up of study centres, vehicle of curricular programmes, live contact with teachers, and so on. On the basis of the recommendations of the working group, the Union Government prepared a draft bill for the establishment of a National Open University, but due to some reasons the progress was delayed.

In 1985, the Union Government made a policy statement for establishment of a national open university. A committee was constituted by the Ministry of Education to chalk out the plan of action of the National Open University. On the basis of the report of the Committee, the Union Government introduced a bill in the Parliament. In August 1985 both the Houses of the Parliament passed the bill. Subsequently, the National Open University came into existence on 20 September 1985. It was named after late Prime Minister, Indira Gandhi.

In 1989, the first convocation was held and more than 1,000 students graduated and were awarded their diplomas. IGNOU audio-video courses were first broadcast by radio and television in 1990 and IGNOU awarded degrees received full recognition by the University Grants Commission in 1992 as being equivalent to those of other universities in the country.

In 1999 IGNOU launched the first virtual campus in India, beginning with the delivery of computer and information sciences courses via the Internet.

Vision and Mission

Vision

IGNOU, the National Resource Centre for Open and Distance learning (ODL), with international recognition and presence, shall provide seamless access to sustainable and learner-centric quality education, skill upgradation and training to all by using innovative technologies and methodologies and ensuring convergance of existing systems for massive human resource required for promoting integrated national development and global understanding.

Mission

To advance frontiers of knowledge and promote its dissemination through sustainable Open and Distance Learning systems, seamlessly accessible to all, including those hitherto unreached, from among whom the leaders and innovators of tomorrow will emerge, the university shall:

- Strengthen the development of the National Resource Center as a proactive role model for high-quality and learners-centric Open and Distance Learning system;
- Share professional capabilities and resources to improve standards of distance education in the country;
- Periodically assess and accredit institutions of Open and Distance learning to promote centers of excellence in the country;
- Develop networks, using emerging technologies and methods, with global reach for effective programme delivery;
- Provide an intelligent and flexible system of education to meet the challenges of access and equity and work towards development of a knowledge society;
- Forge convergence of all systems and work for seamless education across national boundaries to develop global collaboration and partnership;
- Take educational to the hitherto unreached and promote community participation for local development through life-coping skills;
- Provide specific need-based education and training opportunities for continuous professional development and skill upgradation to in-service professional and
- Strive towards continuous development of methods and strategies for research and development for generation of knowledge in frontier areas including open and distance learning.

Strategies to Achieve the Mission

IGNOU has both short term as well as long term strategies to achieve its mission and realize its vision. The elements of the action plan to achieve the objectives are:

1. Total Quality Assurance
2. Increasing Enrollment
3. Strengthening the Faculty
4. Widening areas of study
5. Research and Scholarship
6. Reaching the Unreached
7. Effective Student Support Services
8. Strengthening Extension Education
9. Electronic Media in Education
10. International Impact
11. Building Dynamism in the System

Organisation and Governance

The President of India, the visitor of the university, is the highest authority of the University. The Board of Management is the chief executive body of the University. It is empowered by the statutes to look after the management and administration, the revenue, finances and property of the University as well as conducting all academic and administrative affairs. The Academic Council is the apex academic body which decided the academic policies on methods of instruction, evaluation and improvement in academic standards. It also provides guidance and supervision to research activities in the University. The Finance Committee advises the University on all financial matters, fixing the limits for the total recurring and non-recurring expenditure for the year. It also reviews the grants from government, income and resources of the University. It also examines the accounts and scrutinizes the expenditure of the University. The Planning Board is responsible for the design and formulation of priorities for academic programmes offered by the University. It also advises the Board of Management and the Academic Council on any matter that it deem necessary for the fulfillment of the objectives of the University. The Research Council is responsible for the planning, designing, organizing and monitoring of research programmes. The Schools of Studies are the basic academic units responsible for the conceptualization, design and development of academic programmes. Every School of Study has a Board that oversees the academic activities of the Schools. The School Board is chaired by the Director of the School.

The officers of the University include the Vice Chancellor, the Pro-Vice Chancellors, the Directors of School/Divisions/Centres/Institutes, the Registrars, the Finance Officer and the Librarian. The Vice Chancellor is the Chief Executive Officer of the University and is the ex-officio Chairperson of the Board of Management, the Academic Council, the Planning Board, the Research Council and the Finance Committee.

Schools of Studies

1. School of Agriculture
2. School of Computer and Information Science
3. School of Education
4. School of Engineering and Technology
5. School of Extension and Development Studies
6. School of Foreign Language
7. School of Gender and Development Studies
8. School of Humanities
9. School of Inter Disciplinary Studies
10. School of Journalism and New Media Studies
11. School of Law
12. School of Management Studies
13. School of Performing and Visual Arts
14. School of Sciences
15. School of Social Sciences
16. School of Social Work
17. School of Translation Studies
18. School of Tourism and Hospitality Management
19. School of Vocational Educational and Training
20. School of Continuing Education
21. School of Health Sciences

Divisions

1. Academic Coordination Division
2. Computer Division
3. Construction and Maintenance Division
4. Finance and Accounts Division
5. International Division
6. Library and Documentation Division

7. Material Production and Distribution Division
8. Planning and Development Division
9. Regional Services Division
10. Student Evaluation Division
11. Student Registration Division

Institutes, Consortia, Centers, and Chairs

1. Staff Training and Research Institute of Distances Education (STRIDE)
2. Inter University Consortium for Technology Enabled Flexible Education and Development
3. Electronic Media Production Centre (EMPC)
4. National Centre for Disability Studies
5. National Centre for Innovation in Distance Education (NCIDE)
6. National ODL Centre for Local Governance
7. Indira Gandhi Centre for Freedom Struggle Studies.

Academic Programmes

IGNOU is offering 228 academic professional, vocational, awareness generation and skill oriented programmes of study at the level of Certificate, Diploma, Bachelor's Degree. Master's Degree and Doctoral Degree through the Schools of Studies. There are numbers of new programmes under development. The focus of the programmes is to meet the various academic and employment needs of the people, specially of the disadvantaged sections of Society. By providing high quality learning materials to learners IGNOU has succeeded in raising the standards of higher education in the Country.

Instructional System

The University provides multi-channel, multi media teaching/learning packages for instruction and self-learning. The different components used for teaching/learning include self-instructional print and audio-video materials, radio and television broadcasts, face-to-face counseling/tutoring, laboratory and hands-on experience, teleconferencing, video conferencing, interactive radio counseling, interactive multimedia CD-ROM and internet based learning, and the use of mobile phones for instant messaging. For courses in streams like sciences, computer science, nursing, medical sciences, education and engineering and technology, arrangements have been made to enable students to attend intensive practical classes/practice teaching at select study centres/work centers/ programme centers. While the traditional distance education delivery through print and study centre support is being strengthened, the University is strengthening the development of interactive multimedia content and learner support through video-conferencing and web-based platform by utilizing the internet. The design of the instructional system as well as teacher and learner capacity building are facilitated by the different Schools, Divisions and Centres of the University.

Learner Support Services

The University has an extensive nation-wide network of Regional Centres and Learner Support Centres, including Work Centres and Programme Study Centres, through which it reaches out to its learners. The University has also established tele-learning centres at its Regional Centres. Depending on the requirement, the University collaborates with private entrepreneurs to provide work experience and tele-learning facilities to its learners. Interactive radio counseling is conducted from the studio in the University as well as from 37 FM radio stations across the country. Interactive lectures and counseling is available to learners through EduSat, at the terminals (SITs), as well as through a few DTH platforms. A major quality intervention achieved during the period was the introduction of the Student/Learner Satisfaction Survey, implemented with the objective of gathering inputs from sampled learners about the performance of the University and the benefits they received from the IGNOU system.

Evaluation Mechanism

At IGNOU, a three-tier mechanism of evaluation is followed:

- Self-evaluation, through devices built into the course material (this is for self-assessment only);
- Continuous evaluation, through any combination of theory-based assignment, practical assignments, project works, log books and contact programmes;
- Term-end evaluation, through examinations, which are conducted at about 850 centres all over the country and overseas twice a year, in June and December. In some of the post Graduate

programmes with a project component, the evaluation process also includes a viva-voce.

Accreditation and Recognition

IGNOU is granted the authority to confer degrees by the IGNOU Act 1985. IGNOU is also recognised as a Central University by the University Grants Commission of India (UGC). The Association of India Universities (AIU) recognises IGNOU conferred degrees as on par with the degrees conferred by its members. All India Council for Technical Education (AICTE) recognises the Master of Computer Applications and Master of Business Administration programmes of IGNOU.

In 1993, IGNOU was designated by the Commonwealth of Learning (COL) as its first Centre of Excellence for Distance Education empowered "to actively participate in Commonwealth co-operative endeavours to identify, nurture, and strengthen open learning institutions throughout the Commonwealth, particularly in the Third World.."

IGNOU also operates as an accreditor for Open University and distance education systems in India through the Distance Education Council (DEC). Authority to do so is granted under IGNOU Act 1985. Since then DEC, as an apex agency, was responsible for recognizing ODL institutes in India. It was mandatory for all institutions to seek approval of the DEC for all existing and new programmes offered through distance made. From May 2013 IGNOU through notification repealed and deleted the statute that provisioned for DEC. From this time the UGC has become a regulatory authority for higher education through open and distance mode. As a result instead of requiring DEC recognisation, approval of UGC is required. The Open Universities which are already recognized by DEC are to follow the same guidelines as given by DEC.

Strengths of OU System

1. OU system has provided greater access to higher education for working people, women and persons residing in remote and inaccessible areas. 41 per cent of the students through distance education at the tertiary level are women as compared to 32.5 per cent in the conventional system. The proportion of Scheduled Castes and Scheduled Tribes enrolled in distance

education compares favourably with their proportion in higher education. 68 per cent of IGNOU's enrolments is in the age group of 25+ and a majority of its students are employed adults.

2. Evidence on the effectiveness of distance education programmes indicates that that they frequently show economies as compared with the conventional face to face education. Though the initial costs of establishing Open Universities more than conventional universities, as enrolment grows per capita cost of distance education at the tertiary level is about 25-30 per cent of the per capita cost of conventional university education.
3. Relaxed entry qualification have enabled a large number of students with no formal qualifications to enroll in undergraduate and professional programmes offered by open universities and correspondence institutes. It is significant that more than 25,000 students, without school leaving qualifications, have been enrolled in IGNOU's Bachelor's Degree programme so far.
4. IGNOU and other universities have been successful in restructuring the undergraduate programme in accordance with UGC's guidelines to provide for multi-disciplinary foundation courses, core courses and application oriented components.
5. Open University is introducing courses on the basis of identified manpower needs, which has resulted in diversification of courses to cater to the requirements of different sections of society in urban and rural areas.
6. In terms of content of courses, structure and use of instructional media, open university programmes make a decisive break from the pattern followed by the conventional system. The distance education system is learner based and enables students to learn at their own pace and convenience at their homes and workplaces. It provides flexibility in combination of courses which encourages inter-disciplinary studies.
7. Distance education courses are modular in structure, permit accumulation of credits, provide for multiple entry and exit and continuous evaluation and feedback.
8. Distance education institutes are utilizing the physical and human resources of the existing educational institutions to minimize their costs. Open universities have an extensive network of regional and study centers which provide support to students near place of residence.

As stated by the founder Vice-Chancellor of IGNOU, the establishment of IGNOU is an important milestone in the development of higher education in the country. It is hoped the University will play a leadership role in strengthening open distance education in the country. The University's innovative and high quality education will help not only its own students, but also the students of the conventional universities. The University has great potential to equalize opportunities to take higher education to the door steps of the people.

IGNOU at a Glance (2015)

Programmes on offer	228
Students Registered in 2014-2015 (Fresh and re-registration)	7, 42,426
Students on rolls	28, 10,958
Schools of studies	21
Regional center	67
Learner support centers	2,981
Academic counselors	43,785
Students awarded degrees/diplomas till 28th Convocation	1, 91,818
Audio/Video Programmes produced	2,334/4,499

8

Korea National Open University, Korea

Korea National Open University (KNOU), is a national university of South Korea, which provides distance learning programmes in Korean for more than 180,000 students. It was established in 1972 as a branch faculty of Seoul National University, with 2-year junior college courses. In 1982, KNOU was separated from SNU and established as a national university, launching programmes for 4-year undergraduate degrees. As of 2009, the university has 46 offices and regional learning centres nationwide, and domestic cable television channel (OUN) for broadcasting lectures. It provides accredited bachelor's and master's degree for various fields, as well as non-degree qualifications such as diplomas and certificates, or life-long learning units.

With more than 180,000 students enrolled, including 700 postgraduate students, KNOU is the first distance and lifelong educational institution of South Korea, and the largest educational institution in the country by enrollment. Since its foundation, more than 500,000 students have been enrolled, and 350,000 students graduated from the university.

Objectives

The mission of the KNOU is to cultivate the talents needed by the country and society through higher education and create an open society of study to contribute to the development of lifelong education. The University's main objectives are (1) to expand the opportunities for higher education, (2) to improve the quality of education, and (3) to provide education to senior citizens and physically disabled persons.

The University has four Colleges:

1. College of Liberal Arts

2. College of Social Science
3. College of Natural Science
4. College of Education

It has also eighteen Graduate Schools:

1. Department of Practical English
2. Department of Practical Chinese
3. Department of Japanese Language and Culture
4. Department of French Language and Culture
5. Department of Law
6. Department of Public Administration
7. Department of Management
8. Department of Media Arts and Culture Contents
9. Department of Agriculture and Life Science
10. Department of Home Economics
11. Department of Computer Science
12. Department of e-Learning
13. Department of Bioinformatics
14. Department of Environmental Health Systems
15. Department of Nursing
16. Department of Lifelong Education
17. Department of Youth Education
18. Department of Early Childhood Education

Academic Unit

Undergraduate	22 Departments and 2 Faculties in 5 Colleges
Graduate	18 Departments in 1 Graduate School
Graduate School of Business Administration	8 Majors

Enrolled Students Number (As of April 1, 2014)

Undergraduate	142,332
Graduate	1,975
Graduate School of Business Administration	101
Prime College	814
Part-time enrollment programme	395
Non-degree programme	5,796
Total	151,413

* The numbers of Part-time enrollment and Non-degree programme are as of Academic year 2013.

Number of Members (As of April 1, 2014)

Professors	151
Professors Emeriti	33
Visiting Professors	4
Adjunct Professors	2
Full-time lecture Professors	5
Researchers	17
Teaching Assistants	140
Lecturers (part-time)/Semester	2,537
Tutors (part-time)/Semester	453
Administrative staff	531
Total	**3,873**

Instructional Media

All courses are supplied with educational lecture through media, along with text books (1 course, 1 medium).

Types of Educational Media

Textbooks and workbooks: Written by the faculty of this university and other well-known domestic universities, textbooks feature detailed and professional contents. On the other hand, workbooks forming one of a pair with textbooks contain summarized core items, supplementary learning materials, and exercise for self-evaluation; they are designed to promote learning effects.

TV: TV lecture is a teaching medium that externally represents Korea National Open University; it is designed not only for the students of Korea National Open University but also for general audiences. Lectures provided by the Open University can be taken through the Open University TV (OUN) channel of Cable TV and satellite TV. Since March 2009, high-definition TV lectures have been provided through IPTV (Internet Protocol Television).

IPTV

This is a service wherein broadcasting programmes are provided to TV receivers through the Information Superhighway (Internet). It is a new media that provides real-time broadcasting in the same manner as in cable or satellite TV or two-way multimedia services that allow viewers to view their desired programmes on the VOD system at the desired time.

Audio: Audio lectures are provided for language study courses, which require repeated learning. Lectures are provided through the Internet. Its merits include the availability of MP3 files for downloading to enable the students to study while on the move or while performing other works.

Multimedia: This type of lecture maximizes learning efficiency using video, text, and various visual materials based on e-learning tools. Lectures are given in the form of video lecture + PPT type, audio lecture + PPT type, and video type. It enables sequential learning by providing preparations for lessons, main lecture, exercises, and reference materials.

WBI (Web-Based Instruction): These are e-learning lectures wherein various teaching activities are carried out based on the web. Various multimedia materials are used including video, audio, and animation. Students actively participate in team projects and online discussions. Moreover, through the support of tutors, the limits of remote media are transcended; thus activating mutual interaction between students and instructors.

> LOD service: This is a service through which all types of lectures (TV, multimedia, audio, and WBI) can be taken through the Internet. Students can take lectures anytime, anywhere as long as Internet connection is available. All lectures can be downloaded in video or audio files and stored in PMP so that students can study even while they are on the move.

> Mobile learning (U-KNOU service): Mobile learning is a learning method that uses mobile as the 4th- generation educational media following radio, TV, and Internet. It best embodies the U-Campus. The U-KNOU service pertains to the mobile learning service provided only by the open university; students can take all lectures excluding web lectures anytime, anywhere using their mobile phones.

Tutoring

Purpose

(a) To establish a learner-oriented teaching and learning system and enhance quality of education.

(b) To complement the shortcomings of non-interactive distance education.

(c) To prevent students from dropping out, and to give motivation for continuous study and learning

Types of Tutors

(a) Department tutors
(b) Cyber tutor

Tutor Management

(a) evaluations (Monthly, Midterm and Final evaluations)
- Target: Department tutor, cyber tutor
- Evaluation criteria
  (i) Qualitative evaluation: Knowledge (Quality of tutoring and professional knowledge about course), technique (Student management skills and computer utilization skills), attitude (integrity, tolerance)
  (ii) Evaluated by professors from each department

(b) Tutor monitoring: Provides feedback for Dept. of Schooling after monitoring of each tutor from each college
- student per college will be selected to be monitored.

Mentoring

This is a learner support programme designed to ensure successful school life for freshmen or transferees. Under this programme, a mentor (a senior who has started studying earlier) provides guidance and assistance through the online and offline systems to freshmen or transferees who need help based on his/her study experience and know-how.

Roles of Mentors

(a) Share learning method know-how.
(b) Promote basic understanding of the school courses.
(c) Provide information on academic affairs and use of the learner support service.

Mentoring Qualifications

Mentor: Korea National Open University students who have studied for at least 2 years or graduates of the university

Mentees: Freshmen or transferees for the relevant year

Roles of Mentors

- Sharing learning methods and skills
- Giving information on major school matters and the use of student supporting services
- Helping basic understanding of the curriculum of each department

Status of Mentoring (as of the 1st semester of 2011)

Number of Personnel			*No. of Mentees per Mentor*
No. of Mentors	*No. of Mentees*	*Total*	
1,523	10,101	11,624	6.7

Effects of Mentoring

(a) Mentor: Strengthen the leader's competence and promote self-esteem and pride.

(b) Mentees: Help improve adaptation to school, motivate them in studying, improve school performance, and promote sentimental stability.

Application for and Matching of Mentors and Mentees

Technology Use

The University uses www, CD-ROM, etc to support learning materials. KNOU launched its own TV Channel in 1996. In 2007, KNOU merged e-learning centre and Educational Media Development Centre into Digital Media Centre. It produces course materials on video, web and multimedia. KNOU uses different types of electronic media such as TV, cable TV, IPTV, Multimedia, Web, Audio.

Student Support

Student support services play an important role in imparting quality education to distance learners. The University has well structured student support services. The University delivers its courses through different types of lectures using TV, VCD, Internet, Radio and face-to-face lectures. It also provides online supplementary materials for effective learning. The University conducts summer and winter schools for weak students in which video conference method is used. These schools are conducted at University headquarters and regional centres. The full-time faculty members travel around regional centres in each semester to offer special lectures and to provide individual support. The University provides free learning materials to the disabled students and electronic textbooks to visually impaired students. Translation software translates written material into audio form.

Student Union Activities

Purpose

To establish a student friendly school environment through autonomous activities and self-management

Structure and Activities

Nationwide Student Union

- An organization representing all students
- Composed of executives, 13 regional student unions, college student unions, nationwide student club association
- Nationwide student union leader: Elected directly through OMR cards at final exam time

Regional Student Union

- Plans and operates various events in the region
- Makes suggestions to the nationwide student union and KNOU after collecting various opinions from students in the regional campus

Study Clubs

- General clubs
  - There are about 300 clubs for general hobbies, e.g., folk music, orchestra, soccer and etc.
  - Number of general clubs at regional campus
- Study clubs
  - Self-taught clubs which compliment face to face education
  - There are about 1,200 throughout the nation

Number of Study Clubs

Department	Number	Department	Number
Korean Language and Literature	103	Tourism	29
English Language and Literature	90	Agricultural Sciences	25
Chinese Language and Literature	53	Home Economics	82
French Language and Literature	1	Computer Science	56
Japanese Studies	48	Information Statistics	9
Law	43	Environmental Health	35
Public Administration	18	Nursing	14
Economics	18	Education	168
Management	65	Youth Education	137
International Trade	22	Early Childhood Education	118
Media Arts and Sciences	40	Culture and Liberal Arts	27

Credit for Social Volunteer Activities

Purpose

To enhance the quality of education through developing the social contributions of KNOU

Method

- Students who volunteered can achieve 2 credits.
- Students can volunteer 30 hours or more at a facility or organization designated by KNOU or at KNOU

Number of Graduates from KNOU

1990	65,649
1991	11,007
1992	10,384
1993	10,604
1994	10,039
1995	13,517
1996	15,909
1997	16,988
1998	19,189
1999	23,424
2000	22,551
2001	26,730
2002	25,565
2003	18,725

In terms of quality in education, KNOU is running under the assumption that distance education is no less effective than classroom teaching in the conventional universities. Distance educators contend that by delivering lectures using advanced ICT could be more effective than education in the conventional universities. However, the behaviour of prospective applicants and the students got admitted to the KNOU since the early 2000s revealed otherwise; the applicants for the freshmen has diminished, since 2001, notwithstanding the low tuition fee in the KNOU. They were concerned and dissatisfied with the quality and reputation of KNOU. The KNOU needs to do its best to improve quality of education. Not indulging in the illusion that large number of students guarantees prosperous university with successful future, it should always concentrate in improving quality. Students are more concerned about the prestige of their qualifications and the status of the institutions from which degrees were awarded. KNOU should well remember this.

Institute of Distance Education (IDE)

Originally founded in 1977 as Institute of Correspondence Education, IDE with it new name, has developed a lot in terms of research competencies. The main objective of IDE include achieving quality assurance in adult learners, promoting professionalism in research on distance education and developing innovations in the working of KNOU.

Two types of research are conducted in IDE—long term research and short term research. Research studies conducted by IDE from 1996 to 2006 number 153. These research areas can be largely classified into the following 9 areas:

1. Policy Development and Management
2. Educational Media: Selection and Development
3. Teaching Learning Methods
4. Quantitative Research
5. Curriculum
6. Learner Support and Counselling
7. Lifelong Learning
8. International Comparative Studies
9. Student Evaluation

Most of the research studies conducted by IDE's scholars are in the areas of KNOU's functioning and their findings are used for improving KNOU's working methods.

IDE strives to keep enhancing and improving the research competency and strength in many aspects. For this it has step up recent by the strategies to be pursued during the coming decade.

Presently several open universities are facing several key challenges such as low retention rate of students and high dropout rates. The role of institutional research becomes important to know reasons for these problems. IDE is concentrating on this problem, besides others. IDE is also trying to contribute to more systematic research for the quality assurance of KNOU.

KNOU is playing a significant role in national higher education. It is enabling people to upgrade and update their qualifications. It provides great opportunities for acquiring new skills and values. Distance education has achieved an impressive quantitative and qualitative growth. Modern distance education has proved to be an innovative way of providing higher education to a large segment of population.

9

National Open University of Nigeria

The National Open University of Nigeria is a Federal Open and Distance Learning (ODL) institution, the first of its kind in the West African sub-region. It is Nigeria's largest tertiary institution in terms of student numbers and is popularity referred to as 'NOUN'.

The National Open University was initially established on 22 July 1983 as springboard for open and distance learning in Nigeria. It was suspended by the government on 25 April 1984. However, its resuscitation was began on the 12th of April 2001 by the former President of Nigeria, Gen. Olusegun Obasanjo. At take off of the university, pioneer student enrollment stood at 32,400.

Organization

In 2011, NOUN had about 57,759 students. The Vice Chancellor is Prof. Vincent Tenebe. The National Open of Nigeria operates from its Administration Headquarters in Lagos, Nigeria, with Study Centers throughout the country. It offers over 50 programmes and 750 courses.

NOUN does not provide lectures to students in normal classrooms except some certain study centers, primarily due to constraints known to the University alone and the challenges usually faced by a developing tertiary institution. The study centre in Lagos for instance provides lectures to all its Law undergraduates and supplies necessary course materials to all students after the payment of tuition fees. All courses offered have been accredited by the National Universities Commission (NUC).

The Register serves as the Secretary to Council and Senate bodies. The Registry Department's primary responsible is to provide support services in the General Administration of the University with emphasis on Council affairs, Senate matters, recruitment of Staff, Student's admission/welfare. Staff welfare and other related activities.

Schools and Courses

School of Science and Technology

Post Graduate Programmes

- Information Technology
- Digital Communication
- Mobile (Wireless) Communication Technology
- HIV/AIDS
- Agriculture and Extension

Undergraduate Programmes

- Mathematics
- Computer and Mathematics (Combined Hons)
- Computer Science
- Data Management
- Communications Technology
- Agriculture Extension and Management
- Nursing Science
- Community Health
- Environmental Science and Resource Management (ESM)
- Financial Mathematics
- Physics
- Chemistry
- Biology

School of Health Science

- Nursing
- Community Health/Public Health

School of Arts and Social Sciences

- French and International Studies
- Mass Communication
- Peace, Conflict and Resolution
- English Language

- Economics
- Political Science

School of Law

- Law LL
- Law LLM

School of Education

Undergraduate Programmes

- Agric Science
- Biology
- Chemistry
- Computer Science
- Physics
- Integrated Sciences
- Mathematics
- Business Education
- Primary Education
- Early Childhood Education
- English
- French

Masters Programmes

- Admin and Planning
- Science Education
- Education Technology

School of Management Sciences

Undergraduate Courses

- Cooperative Science
- Entrepreneurial and Business Management
- Accounting in collaboration with the Institute of Chartered Accountants of Nigeria

Post Graduate courses

- Financial Management
- Business Administration
- Public Administration
- Master of Business Administration

- Public Administration
- Public Sector Management.

Centre for Life-Long Learning and Workplace Training

- Diploma Programmes
- Business Communication
- Medical Office Practice
- Entrepreneurship
- Financial Management
- Marketing

Academic Certificates Programmes

- Dental Office Practice
- Computer Literacy
- Returning Students
- Medical Office Practice
- Financial Management
- Entrepreneurship
- Marketing

Students

Requirements

A diverse range of students from all walks of life are attracted to the National Open University of Nigeria just like others prominent Open Universities such as the Open University of United Kingdom (OU); for most courses there are no stringent entry requirements other than the ability to study at an appropriate level such as the West African Examination, and other National Diplomas to quality for a Direct entry admission. Though most postgraduate courses require evidence of previous study and/or equivalent life experience. This fundamental open admissions policy makes undergraduate university study accessible to all.

Undergraduates

While most of those studying are mature students, an increasingly large proportion of new undergraduates are aged between 17 and 25, the reduction in financial support for those attending traditional universities, coupled with the use of technologies such as and YouTube that appeal to this demographic, is believed to be behind this growth.

Immunity to Strikes

Another reason is the Act of Parliament which established the University prohibiting any form of union either within staffs or students. This has made the NOUN to be unaffected by strikes such as the ASSU strikes (which lasted for eight months) in Nigeria which ultimately extends students course duration in school unnecessarily, NOUN students have always and will continue to be immune to any form of strike.

National Youths Service Corps and the Nigerian Law School

The NOUN is making efforts to ensure its graduation below age 30 (the maximum age limit) participate in the National Youth Service Corps and Law graduates proceed to the Nigerian Law School. However, efforts have of recent, been materialized.

Rankings

Latest results of University Rankings released by Ranking Web of Universities (popularity known as Webometrics) revealed another list of 100 Universities in Nigeria for 2015. Just as done in every other web ranking, webometrics ranking 2015 adopted search queries from search engines to rank the top universities which the National Open University ranked 23rd.

Convicted Prison Inmates

The decision of the management and senate of National Open University Nigeria (NOUN) to establish study centers in some of the nation's prisons has started yielding fruits as three inmates were among the over 7,000 that recently graduate from the 13-year-old institute.

Technological Platforms

NOUN ilearn

The National Open University of Nigeria in its effort to take education to the doorstep of the Nigerian populace irrespective of their social status and the developing economy of Nigeria has deployed and implemented iLearn portal technology to enhance student's learning experience. The NOUN iLearn platform has been created to ease access to excellent quality education. The platform provides amongst many, the following:

Online class discussion organized by NOUN facilitators thereby creating a virtual classroom environment.

Faculty for students to get answers to any questions or areas of difficulty pertaining to their course of study.

Networking and collaboration tools to help in community of interaction among students, facilitators, academic staff and faculty members.

Better study tools such as the smart e-Book Digitized lecture video and audio materials for an enhanced student' learning experience available on the platform.

Access to assignments, quizzes and self-study assessment tools.

Examination

The university administers the Computer-Based-Test (CBT) form of examination to its students in their first and second years. However, Law undergraduates participate in the standard pen-On-Paper examinations (POP) beginning from their first year of admission, with LAW111-Legal Methods in First Semester of the first year.

Other graduates also participate in the CBT system of examination in their fist and second years and commence the POP examination from their first year till the end of their respective course durations. The POP examination system applied Post Graduate students also.

The CBT system of examination has however been criticised by some of the students. The CBT examination is in two categories; the multiple choice questions and fill in the gap—which is the most dreaded examination type by students all around the world.

Assessment

Tutor-Marked Assignments (TMAs) are continuous assessment in form of Tutor Marked Assignment and it accounts for 30 per cent of students total score. Students are expected to answer at least four TMAs, three of which must be answered and submitted before students sit for the end of course examination.

Final Examination and Grading

With examination written successfully, The 'end of course examinations' would earn students 70 per cent which would be added to their TMA score (30%). Theme for this examination is always communicated to students.

Facilities

E-library: The NOUN operates an e-library at the headquarters, Victoria Island, Lagos, Nigeria which all students have access to after providing a valid student's identity card. Students access to both Internet facilities, books, journals, projects, thesis of past students and other educational materials.

Radio Station: The radio station broadcasts at the frequency 105.9 NOUN FM. Mass Communication students also have the opportunity to intern at the studio which broadcasts on all working days.

E-courseware: The NOUN also provides a platform for students that needs to access its database of educational materials strictly for educational purpose rather than financial or commercial purpose. Books can be downloaded in PDF formats at no coast.

10

National University of Distance Education, Spain

The **National University of Distance Education**, known in Spanish as Universidad National de Education a Distancia (UNED), is a distance learning and research university founded in 1972 and is the only university run by the central government of Spain. It has headquarters in Madrid, Spain, with campuses in all Spanish autonomous communities.

UNED combines traditional onsite education with distance learning programmes. With over 2,60,000 Students, UNED is the largest university in Spain and the second largest in Europe.

UNED was founded in 1972 following the idea of the UK's Open University to provide quality higher and continuing education opportunities to all through a distance education system. It awards the same qualifications as other Spanish universities and has the same entry requirements. This implies that it is not "Open". Even though the study is at distance, admissions are as strict as for "onsite" education and exams are supervised as in the other Spanish universities. It is nationwide in scope, applies the most advanced teaching technologies and has a wide social unfluence with radio and TV programming.

UNED is a university where distance is no object for the fact that, through its educational methodology, UNED is the only university that offers the possibility of obtaining formal qualifications adapted to the European Higher Education Area (EHEA) from anywhere in the world. Likewise, UNED is the only university with centers in the Americas, Africa, Europe and all the Autonomus Communities of Spain; finally, training at UNED is carried out using new technologies, principally the internet.

UNED developed very rapidly. Initial planning began in 1968. A formal planning committee was established in May 1971. The University's charter was granted in August 1972; a Rectar was appointed in September 1972 with a brief to have UNED functioning by February 1973, initial courses were approved by the Ministry of Education and Science in December 1972, and the first group of 11,400 students on Admissions, law and latter courses were enrolled in February 1973.

UNED is equivalent in every way to conventional universities in Spain. Its degrees are of equal status; like the Conventional Universities, it offers discipline-based courses with fixed programmes of courses, without electives; and students are able to transfer credits between UNED and other universities.

UNED was established with three groups of students in mind: those unable to begin or to complete higher education; those living in remote areas; and those ambitious for more qualifications.

UNED's students tend to be older than those in traditional Spanish universities; nearly all work full time; most are married; and those come mainly from the professional and mid-executive ranks, with the majority-having some form of academic qualifications. In a survey, the three most common reasons given by students as a reason for studying were to improve professional knowledge, improve job prospects, and broaden cultural knowledge.

The majority of students live in Spain. About one percent are resident in other countries, mostly in Western Europe. Within Spain, the relative distribution of students appears to be affected by the degree of industrialization and urbanization, the location of good regional study center and the existence of a local conventional university.

Objectives

UNED was created on the basis of two different main approaches to distance education. On the: (a) individual study and individual non-contiguous tuition relying on open course materials produced for large groups of students, and (b) The parallelism with resident study, usually class or group teaching face-to-face as a regular element. Thus, UNED combined the large-scale type of distance teaching university, with its central headquarters, where the production, distribution of materials and students evaluation are concentrated, with decentralized network of study centers, which introduces human interactive element into highly depersonalized methodology.

UNED has the following formal objectives:

- to provide higher education at home, equivalent to that provided by the conventional universities to all those who missed their first educational opportunity or were unable to attend present institutions of learning without disrupting their normal occupations or because of distance, sickness, rigid working timetable etc.
- to substitute the free learning offered in the traditional universities to those who for some reason or other, could not attend classes and hence, had to study independently as best as they could.
- to become an effective instrument to the implementation of equal opportunities in higher education in Spain.
- to increase the enrolment capacity to the implementation of Spanish universities.
- to develop a more individualized and student-central system of teaching and learning.
- to contribute to methodological innovation in the Spanish higher education system.

Other informal objectives are:

- a cheaper teaching method than conventional education, measured in terms of audience reached and learning.
- a better use of local resources to support distance learning, especially in zones deprived of educational opportunities.
- a flexible way of teaching and learning, which could enable many professionals to update their knowledge at a high speed and a low cost.

Organisation

Though UNED is similar to other distance teaching universities regarding its objectives, its organisational structure provides a national status directly by the Ministry of Education and Science. The most important organ is the Senate, compared of representatives of their academic and administrative staff, students and study center. In addition to the above, UNED has an important network of study centres, established through the initiative of local corporations, public or private agencies which provide the buildings, equipments, materials and pay for the personnel employed including teacher-tutors. Usually located in small cities where there is no university. The UNED study center is also a cultural centre in the area.

International Presence

UNED's mission is to be present as a center of excellence throughout the world. UNED currently has 61 study centers in Spain and 14 abroad, thanks to the co-operation of local institutions. The centers provide face-to-face sessions with professors once a week. The International centers are in Bata, Bern, Brussels, Buenos Aires, Caracas, Frankfurt, Lima, London, Malabo, Mexico City, Paris and Sao Paulo. Additionally, there are exam points in Bogota, Berlin, New York, Rome and Santiago de Chile.

Teaching Methods

UNED features the most complete and advanced methodology for distance learning, putting a whole range of measures and human resources at the disposal of students to enable autonomous learning tailored to their needs and schedules. Based on the use of active methodologies in which student are the protagonist of their own learning, this system is the underlying concept of the European Higher Education Area (EHEA) for the training of professionals capable of taking up the challenges of the knowledge society.

UNED provides instruction by means of a distance learning modality characterized by the use of a specific didactic methodology. The methodology combines the use of print and audiovisual media with that of new technologies, especially virtual learning communities. There are also various systems of communications between professors and students as well as on-site assistance to students from professors—tutors at the Centers.

This methodology is detailed below:

- Human resources for students support: In the Faculties, teaching teams are responsible for the assessment of learning and the preparation of programmes and teaching materials. The students receive support from professors online, by telephone or via videoconference. Should they wish, students can attend tutorials at the Associated Centers given by specialized tutors.

Associated Centers also facilitate the formation of study and working groups made up of students from the same center. The student can develop those activities through a Virtual Platform (ALF) where the university community can exchange information, material, documents, etc. More than 1,400 public employees make the operation of the university possible and provide the necessary support for teaching and research staff to carry out their work under the most optimal conditions.

- Printed audiovisual and multimedia materials: Printed materials (texts and study guides) specially designed for autonomous learning and a very wide range of audiovisual and multimedia materials develop by UNED (videos, CDs, DVDs). Audiovisual media like radio, educational television and the UNED Channel (online radio and TV-[1] (http://www.Canaluned.com)). UNED students are integrated into a broader virtual community where they have access to various online service that respond to their needs (e.g., virtual courses, virtual study communities and virtual library and administrative department). Each course has its own virtual domain with activities, supplementary materials, self-assessment tools, and chats and forums, allowing students to communicate with teaching staff, tutors and classmates. Students can also join online work and study communities formed by classmates at any Center.
- Carrying out the in-person exams at the Associated Centers: Examinations are written by teaching teams at the Faculties and distributed to all Associated Centers by virtual pouch. All conducted examinations are returned to the corresponding teaching teams for evaluation.

Academic Faculties

Undergraduate

Today, UNED comprises 11 faculties and the following bachelor's degree studies:

- *Higher Technical School of Computer Engineering at UNED*: Bachelor's Degrees in Computer Engineering, Engineering Information Technology.
- *College of Industrial Engineering*: Bachelor's in Electrical Engineering, Industrial Technologies Engineering's, Mechanical Engineering, Industrial Electronics and Automation.

- *Faculty of Science*: Bachelor's Degrees in Environmental Science, Physics, Mathematics, Chemistry.
- *Faculty of Economics and Business Administration*: Bachelor's Degrees in Economics, Business Administration and Management, Tourism.
- *Faculty of Political Science and Sociology*: Bachelor's Degrees in Sociology, Political Science and Public Administration.
- *Faculty of Law*: Bachelor's Degrees in Law, Social work, Juridical Science of Public Administration.
- *Faculty of Education*: Degrees in Social Education, Pedagogy.
- *Faculty of Philology*: Bachelor's Degrees in Spanish Language and Literature, English Studies: Language and Literature and Culture.
- *Faculty of Philosophy*: Bachelor's Degrees in Philosophy, Social and Cultural Anthropology.
- *Faculty of Geography and History*: Bachelor's Degrees in Geography and History, Arts History.
- *Faculty of Psychology*: Degree in Psychology.

Postgraduate

- *Higher Technical School of Computer Engineering at UNED*: Computer Systems and Languages, Advanced Artificial Intelligence: Principles, Methods and Applications, Communication, Networks and Content Management, Systems and Control Engineering.
- *College of Industrial Engineering*: Research in Industrial Technology, Research in Electronic and Industrial Control Engineering, Advanced Manufacturing Engineering, Design Engineering.
- *Faculty of Science*: Chemical Science and Technology, Polymer Science and Technology, Advance Mathematics, Medical Physics of Complex Systems.
- *Faculty of Economics and Business Administration*: Corporate Sustainability and Social, Responsibility.
- Faculty of Political Science and Sociology, Social Problems, Politics and Democracy.
- *Faculty of Law*: Government Intervention in Society, European Union, Fundamental Rights, Security, Insurance Law, Human Rights, Public Finance, Public Policy and Taxation.
- *Faculty of Educational Treatment of Diversity, communication and*

Education on the Internet: From the Information Society to the knowledge Society, Innovation and Research in Education, Training of E.S.O., Bachillerato, F.P. and Language Secondary Teachers, Strategies and technologies for the Teaching function in the Multicultural Society.

- *Faculty of Philology*: Literary and Theatre Training and Research in the European Context. The Classical World and its Influence on Western Culture, Applied English Linguistics, Hispanic Literatures (Catalan, Galician and Basque) in the European Context, Language Science and Hispanic Linguistics, Grammatical and Stylistic Analysis of Spanish, Dictionary Development and Quality Control of the Spanish Lexicon, French and Francophone Studies, Information Technologies and Communication In Language Education and Processing.
- *Faculty of Philosophy*: Theoretical and Practical Philosophy.
- *Faculty of Geography and History*: Advanced Methods and techniques of historical, artistic and Geographic Research, Contemporary Spain in the International context
- *Faculty of Psychology*: Methodology of Behavioural Sciences and Health, Research in Psychology, Psychological Intervention in Development and Education

UNED Continues to be a channel for the cultural and professional development of many adults and as a mean of modernization of country's whole education system

11

Open University of China

The Open University of China was established in Beijing in 1979. Its old name was China Central Radio and TV University (this is still the Chinese name), which reflects its heritage of providing a system of higher education through radio and television. The university is directly under the supervision of the Ministry of Education.

Mission

The OUC upholds the educational philosophy of "Openness, Responsibility, Quality, Diversity and Internationalization". The University is rapidly expanding non-degree continuing education which continuing to develop degree continuing education, integrating modern technology with education.

Supporting Alliances

The OUC established 4 major supporting alliances to help fulfil its historic mission and realise its social values, develop a learning society and fully utilise available high quality social sources. A university supporting alliance was established based on cooperation between OUC and other Universities in China. The University also established an industry supporting alliances, an enterprise supporting alliance and a city supporting alliance. By leveraging the resources and strengthens of these entities, the University will develop various programmes of vocational training, community education and citizen education and promote the construction of learning industries, learning enterprises and learning cities.

The Open University of China is a new style university without walls; open to all members of society. It was established on the basis of the former China Central Radio and TV University (CRTVU) and local Radio and TV Universities, and uses modern information technology. It assigns equal weight to degree and non-degree education. At present, these are 3.59 million registered students, of which 1.05 million are undergraduates and 2.54 million are junior college students. Among them, 2,00,000 are rural students, 1,00,000 are military personal and 6,000 are disabled students The establishment of OUC mark a start of new journey in China.

Structure

In 2009, the open universities in China consisted of Open University of China (OUC), 44 provincial open universities (referring to the open universities established in provinces, autonomous regions, municipalities directly under the central government and cities with economic planning directly supervised by the State Council and other independently established open universities); 933 municipal open universities (referring to 744 branch schools and 159 open universities under the direct administration of the provincial open universities); 1829 Country-level open universities (referring to the open universities under the direct administration of the branch schools).

OUC is a university under direct administration of the Ministry of Education of China. It is an Open University that conducts national modern distance education through various media, such as printed materials, audio-visual materials, multi-media course wares and online courses based on computer networks and satellite TV network.

The preparation for OUC establishment began in February 1978 and it was officially founded in February 1979.

OUC is member of AAOU and ICDE. It has established communicative and cooperative relationships with many distance education institutions in other countries like USA, Canada, Australia, France, Sweden, England, Germany, Korea, Japan, Thailand, etc.

OUC offers 75 majors in 9 disciplines and 24 specialisations including science, engineering, agriculture science, medicine, literature, law, economics, management and education.

By the fall of 2008, there were 30,90,000 active students in the Open Universities in China among whom 29,50,000 were students of junior colleges and undergraduate students, accounting for one tenth of the total enrolment in higher education in the country.

In 2009, there were 2.635 million active students registered in the OUC open education programmes, including 791,100 undergraduates students, 1.7105 million junior college students and 1,61,900 students in the One-College-Student-for-One-Village programme.

At present, it is the largest open and distance education system in the world.

Faculties

OUC has six Faculties:

1. Faculty of Arts and Law
2. Faculty of Economics and Management
3. Faculty of Engineering
4. Faculty of Teacher Education
5. Faculty of Foreign Languages
6. Faculty of Agro Forestry and Medicine.

OUC has many schools addressing to specified groups of learners for degree programmes. Such schools are Bayi School, Zongcan School, and School for the Air Force, School of Tibet and School for the disabled. OUC also has a school of continuing education offering non-degree education programmes.

Courses

In the early years of its existence the CRTVU's courses were transmitted for 33 teaching hours per week nationwide via the microwave network of the CCTV. On 1 July 1986 China Educational TV (CETV) was founded and started to transmit the CRTVU's courses. Presently, the total number of programmes transmitted via both CCTV and CETV per year amounts to 9,000 teaching hours. Local TV and radio stations also transmit some of the CRTVU's courses as well as local TVU's courses.

The CRTVU offers a wide variety of vocational training and continuing education courses at different levels in terms of non-degree education.

Since 1986, the CRTVU cooperated with more than 40 institutions, including government departments, vocational organizations, academic bodies, universities, colleges and large enterprises to run some 60 projects in non-degree education, which resulted about 4 million trainers. In addition, PRTVUs also offered non-degree education courses with a total number of over 30 million trainees.

Technical Framework

The development and widespread application of modern information technology has not only exerted a profound influence on people's methods of production, lifestyles and ways of thinking, it has also had a revolutionary impact on the development of education. The OUC is devoted to integrating technology and education; promoting innovation in education; enhancing educational capacity, quality and management; and promoting educational equality and the sharing of quality education resources. With the assistance if high-level ICT enterprises, the OUC has established a cloud platform for distance education. With the help of high-level online operators, the OUC's headquarters and branches are connected safely and quickly through VPNs, the Internet, the education and research network, the mobile communication network, and the satellite network. Furthermore, the OUC will partner with top-tier terminal manufacturers to develop mobile learning device and make learning accessible to all citizens. All of the above has built a powerful digital platform for distance education, which can provide learning support and services for billions of users.

Learning Model

The OUC devotes to realizing well supported open learning, and is exploring a new learner-centred learning pattern, primarily based on online self-directed learning and supplemented by distance learning support and face-to-face tutorials. Since it is demand-oriented and focuses on developing students' abilities, the OUC is reforming its teaching content and curriculum system, cooperating with industries and enterprises, and developing programmes that embody its characteristics. By improving teaching methods, the OUC is able to provide learners with a large number of high quality online courses, integrating multimedia resources, interactive teaching, learning assessment and learner support. In addition to face-to-face tutorials provided by learning centres all over the country, teachers and students can also achieve real-time communication through a high speed HD two-way video system. Distance learning support and services are thus provided to learners at anytime and anywhere. The evaluation model is also changing from summative assessment to formative assessment.

Credit Bank

The OUC endeavours to promote lifelong learning for all. Accordingly, the university has established a credit bank system that includes functions like credit accreditation, credit transfer, and credit access. Every learner has his own lifelong learning portfolio. Learners can accumulate credits according to the credit accumulation rules that have been put in place. When they accumulate enough credits, they can apply for the corresponding certificates. The credit bank strives to provide a basis for the mutual recognition and transfer of credits between different educational and training institutions. Social members are encouraged to accumulate credits so that degree education and non-degree education can be linked up. By building this kind of "shortcut" to lifelong learning, the OUC is pushing forward the development of a lifelong learning system.

Research Institute of Open and Distance Education

Established in 1985, the Research Institute of Open and Distance Education of the Open University of China (OUC) is China's oldest research institution on distance education. Since 2001, it has assumed the additional function as the Research Division of OUC.

Geared towards the interests of all OU students, the Institute actively pools the wisdom and talent of the experts and the staff members of OUs. Over the past 25 years, it has engaged in research and achieved numerous results in the theory and practice in such fields as distance education, open education, adult education, and the application of educational technology.

As the research arm of OUC, the Institute has undertaken numerous national level research projects since 1986. Such projects include the research on educational mode, curriculum design, teaching mode, administrative mode, support services, as well as quality assurance, and the assessment system of distance education. The research findings have been published in many journals and books. As a result of such sustained academic pursuits, a team of full-time and part-time researchers, which consists of researchers, teachers, administrators and technicians, has emerged. They have gained a solid domestic and international reputation for the quality of their research in distance education.

Since 2008, the Institute has been publishing, on an irregular basis, Currents in Research (internal circulation). The Journal focuses on the latest developments and trends in research in educational technology as well as in open and distance education (ODE). The articles may serve as the rationale and reference for decision-making, strategy planning, curriculum development, technology application, support services, and other research projects of the OUs throughout the country.

Currently, it consists of the Division of Theory and Policy Studies, the Division of Teaching and Management Studies, the Division of Media Technology and Application Studies, the Research Management Office, and the Administrative Office.

The Institute conducted extensive surveys, studied learner support services and published many reports, books and articles. Some of these are: (a) Study on Adult Learning, (b) Social Assessment Study, (c) Study on the reform of Personnel Training Mode, (d) Study on Assurance of Teaching Quality of China Open Universities, (e) Empirical and comparative cost-based-study on Distance Education of Open Universities (f) Study on the Formation of Modern Distance Education Culture.

Some Problems Facing Distance Education

1. There is the problem of access. Individual web- based study is still not possible for most people,
2. Internet access is expensive. Most Chinese citizens-particularly those who would most benefit from distance education, cannot afford it.
3. The lack of locally produced software
4. Online centers are not yet efficiently managed
5. Many DE teachers lack specific training.
6. A relatively small number of students actually graduate from distance education programmes
7. China does suffer at the moment from a lack of infrastructure: inadequate bandwidth; inadequate access to computers; and inadequate software.

Distance education can play a significant role in realising equity in Chinese higher education. There are three opportunity inequities in Chinese higher education: (1) inequity among students from different regions of the country, with students in the eastern part having an advantage over those in the western part, (2) inequity among students from different social groups, with students from rich families having an advantage over those from poor families, (3) inequity caused by competition among institutions due to certain government policies, with some institutions having an advantage over others.

Since distance education is able to overcome the constraints of space and time, it has an important contribution to make in promoting the equity of education opportunities. With the more government support to the radio and television universities at different levels in the country can develop faster, reducing inequity in education.

Chinese distance education started later than that in developed countries, but it is making significant progress in the higher education sector. While there are problems in development and there is much to do before Chinese distance education demonstrates the three characteristics described by Spector and Merrill (2008) effective, efficient and engaging, as Chinese distance educators learn from international colleagues, reflect on their own practices and conduct more research on distance education in the Chinese context, distance education move forward and make its due contribution. As distance education, continues to develop, it will provide more education opportunities to people across China.

12

Open University of Hong Kong

The Open University of Hong Kong (OUHK) is a Hong Kong university providing sub-degree, degree and postgraduate courses leading to awards and qualifications principally through a system of open access and distance education.

The university was initially named Open Learning Institute of Hong Kong (OLIHK). Under the expansion of education in the 1990s in Hong Kong, the establishment of institute introduced distance learning to Hong Kong and set an alternative path of continuing education for its working force. Students are able to adjust the pace of learning according to their own conditions.

As programmes of study are self-financing, there are no financial subsidies from the Hong Kong Government for the university itself. However, full-time students may get grants and loans from the scheme "Financial Assistance Scheme for Post-secondary Students" (FASP), while other distance learning students are able to make special loan arrangements with a bank.

The OUHK has designed many non-distance learning courses, including full-time courses. In 2006-2007 academic year, they also participated the Joint University Programmes Admissions System, which mainly target at secondary school graduates, marked as the only self-financed university under the scheme.

Hong Kong Baptist Hospital became affiliated with the Open University of Hong Kong, which enables nurses to be trained up to the university degree standard. The Hong Kong Sanatorium and Hospital has a School of Nursing, also affiliated with The Open University of Hong Kong.

Milestones

1989	Established by the Hong Kong Government as The Open Learning Institute to offer part-time distance learning degree programmes
1993	Began self-financing
1996	Gained self-accrediting status by the Hong Kong Government
1996	Moved to the permanent Homantin Campus
1997	Granted university status by the Hong Kong Government
1997	Re-titled as The Open University of Hong Kong
2001	Launched the first full-time degree programmes
2008	Opened Homantin Campus Phase Two
2013	Opened Kwai Hing Learning Centre
2014	Opened Jubilee College

Vision

The Open University of Hong Kong strives to be a leader among universities providing learning opportunities by open and flexible education, and to excel as a provider of higher education in general.

Mission

The mission of The Open University of Hong Kong is to make higher education available to all, principally through open and flexible learning.

Key Values

In providing higher education, the University, as a self-financing, non-profit-making organization:

- believes that higher education should be available to all those aspiring to it, regardless of previous qualification, gender, or race;
- recognizes the importance of sustainable and affordable high-quality programmes and courses across disciplines and at a variety of levels to meet the needs of lifelong learners;
- commits itself to excellence in teaching, scholarship, research and public service;
- effectively uses information and communication technologies to support learning;

- appreciates the significance of adjusting its learning processes and procedures to meet the different needs of learners

Governance and Organization

The Court and Council serve as the supreme advisory and governing body of the University respectively. The University is comprised of the following academic and administrative units.

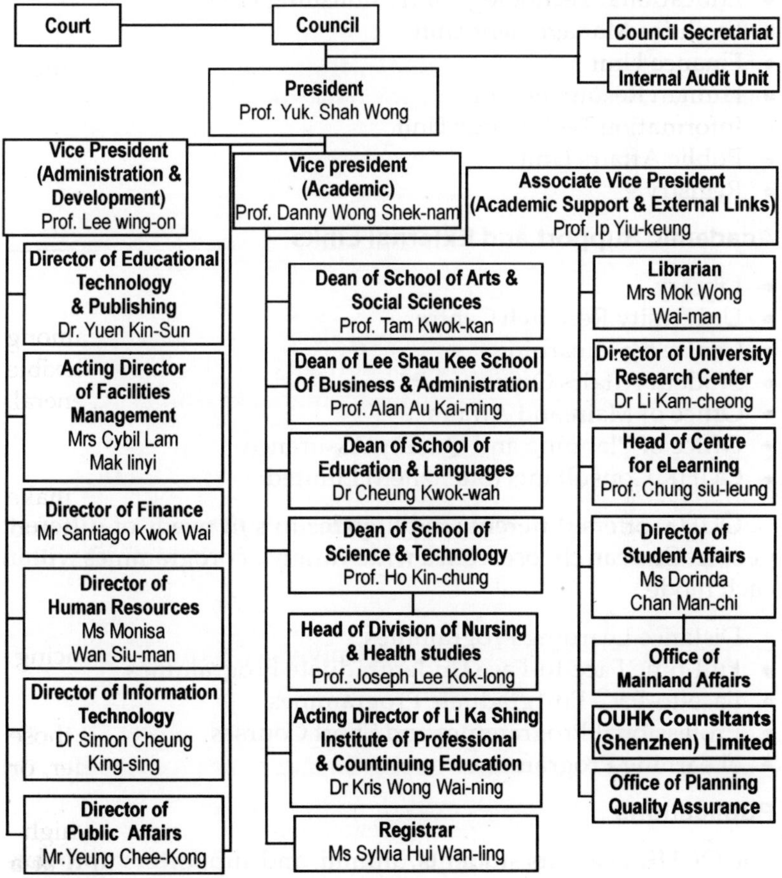

Schools

- School of Arts and Social Sciences
- Lee Shau Kee School of Business and Administration
- School of Education and Languages

- School of Science and Technology
- Division of Nursing and Health Studies, School of Science and Technology
- Li Ka Shing Institute of Professional and Continuing Education (LiPACE)

Administrative Units

- Educational Technology and Publishing Unit
- Facilities Management Unit
- Finance Unit
- Human Resources Unit
- Information Technology Unit
- Public Affairs Unit
- Registry

Academic Support and External Links

- Library
- University Research Centre
- Centre for eLearning
- Student Affairs Office
- Office of Mainland Affairs
- Office of Planning and Quality Assurance
- OUHK Consultants (Shenzhen) Limited

OUHK offers different study modes to suit needs of different people. One can choose from a wide variety of programmes within each mode.

- Distance Learning Programmes
- Full-time Face-to-Face Undergraduate Programmes
- Face-to-Face Postgraduate Programmes
- Professional Programmes and Short Courses
- eLearning Programmes

Publications

The OUHK keeps its students, alumni, and supporters upto date on University news through several printed and online publications.

- Open Link, a quarterly newsletter, features latest development and accomplishment of the University, scholarly activities, student stories and alumni news.

- The monthly e-Bulletin provides a summary of the University's latest news, upcoming events and programme information through its online platform.
- OUHK Annual Report highlights the outstanding achievements of the OUHK and provides all-round information in many different aspects of the OUHK present and future development. The report reflects activities, initiatives, outcomes, and fundraising results for the period from 1 April of the previous year to 31 March of the current year. It also provides an overview of the University's financial performance.
- The University also runs its own publishing company, the OUHK Press.

Strategic Plan

To uphold the vision and mission, OUHK needs to remain competitive and makes every effort to take advantage of the favourable opportunities and overcome the unfavourable threats. As self-financing university OUHK, is among the top choice for students who wish to pursue a degree from the self-financing/ private sector. OUHK continues to provide high quality academic programmes in areas of demand through flexible delivery modes; ensures students' learning experience including extracurricular activities is of high standard; and enhances student support by devoting more resources to it.

The following seven main strategic initiatives are to attain the university goals.

1. Enhancing student support as an integral part of teaching and learning
2. Offering more alternative programmes
3. Exploring blended learning courses
4. Building up research capacity
5. Presenting more postgraduate programmes
6. Extending global activity
7. Consolidating financial position

The successful implementation of strategic plan will be heavily dependent on student enrolment and financial situation in the coming years. Given its past record, OUHK is confident that it will continue to be a leading self-financing institution which offers high quality programmes and student services.

Research

The OUHK established a Centre for Research in Distance and Adult Leaning in 1977 to meet the needs of research and researchers locally, regionally and globally. The Centre's main objective is to develop a distance education and open learning research culture and focus, develop critical mass of staff and capacity building in research and collaboration with other institutions around the world on research activities in open and distance education. As part of its current plan, the centre has embarked on some research activities which particularly interest Hong Kong, East Asia, Asia Pacific regions and other throughout the world who have particular interests in the outcomes of research in distance and adult learning.

The University encourages academic staff to actively participate in research and provides support for the internal and external funding for research and development projects.

13

Open University of Japan

The Open University of Japan (OUJ) was founded in 1983 by the Open University of Japan Foundation, under the auspices of the Ministry of Education, Culture, Sports, Science and Technology, and the Ministry of Internal Affairs and Communications.

It is an accredited educational institution open to all the people in Japan. OUJ utilizes broadcasting media and other means for new and effective ways to meet the needs for lifelong learning. The objectives of the Open University of Japan are to provide a wide range of people with opportunities for obtaining higher education and to promote broadcasting media and other innovative means of education for universities and other higher education institutions.

OUJ has grown to become the largest distance education institution in Japan. To date, over 1,300,000 people have studied at OUJ, with over 83,000 of them graduating with a degree. Taking advantages of terrestrial digital broadcasting and satellite broadcasting, OUJ provides effective broadcast lectures using vivid visuals in high-definition and information content developed by experts in the field.

Milestones

April 1983	The University of the Air (U-Air) was established
April 1985	Undergraduate students were accepted and broadcasting lectures were started
April 1989	The first bachelor's degree was awarded
January 1998	Nationwide broadcasting over CS (communications satellite) digital broadcasting was launched
October 1998	Students enrolled in undergraduate degree programmes were accepted at Study Centers throughout Japan

April 2001	The School of Graduate Studies was established for Master's degree
March 2004	The first master's degree was awarded
December 2006	Terrestrial digital broadcasting service (the Kanto region only) was launched
October 2007	U-Air was renamed as the Open University of Japan (OUJ)
October 2011	Nationwide broadcasting over BS (Broadcast Satellite) digital broadcasting was launched
March 2012	CS (communications satellite) digital broadcasting service was terminated
October 2014	Ph.D. Programme was started

Student Enrollment

Academic Year 2013

Student Type	*Total*
Regular Students	11,858
One-Year Non-Degree Students	17,459
One-Semester Non-Degree Students	14,029
Special Auditing Students	4,648
Total	47,994
Master's Course Students	440
One-Year Non-Degree Master's Course Students	3,765
One-Semester Non-Degree Master's Course Students	1,611
Total	5,816
Faculty of Liberal Arts	
Regular Students	55,717
One-Year Non-Degree Students	17,533
One-Semester Non-Degree Students	7,525
Special Auditing Students	3,459
Total	84,234
School of Graduate Studies	
Master's Course Students	1,159
One-Year Non-Degree Master's Course Students	3,805
One-Semester Non-Degree Master's Course Students	956
Total	5,920
Students Enrolled in Summer Intensive Course	
School Librarianship Certification Program	807
Nurse Qualification Course	496
Total	1,303

Faculty of Liberal Arts

The Faculty of Liberal Arts at OUJ offers courses in a wide range of academic fields to meet the diverse needs of students and the general public, so as to broaden their education and deepen their knowledge in specialized fields that are related to their real lives.

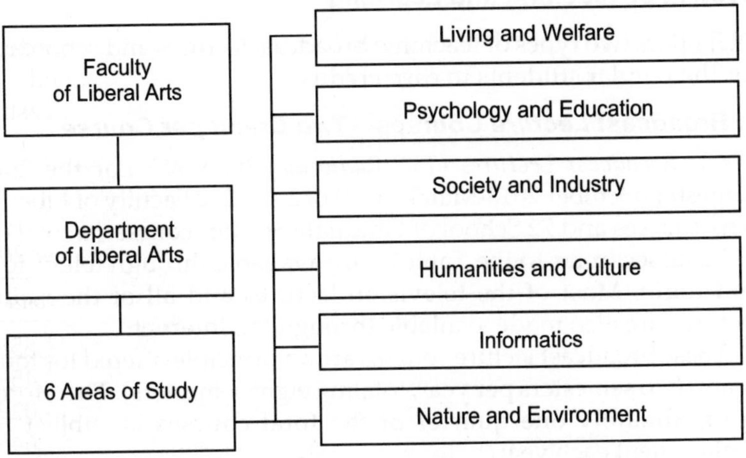

Fig. 14.1: Faculty of Liberal Arts

The following six areas of study are being offered. The students enrolled to acquire a bachelor's degree must select one area of study and earn more than 124 credits including the minimum of 20 credits earned through schooling.

The six areas of study are:

- Living and Welfare
- Psychology and Education
- Society and Industry
- Humanities and Culture
- Informatics
- Nature and Environment

Non-Degree Expert Courses

The "Expert" system, an original OUJ subject group credit certification system, was introduced in the 2006 academic year. Objectives of a subject matter in a given field are achieved through the completion of specific university-designated plan, and this confirms the achievement of a systematic study to that end. With the 2007 revision of the School Education Act, the "certified evaluation and accreditation system" regulations for universities also came into effect. Implemented again in the 2008 academic year, the "Expert" system became the OUJ's response to the "certified evaluation and accreditation system".

System of Teaching and Learning

OUJ offers two types of teaching: broadcast lectures and schooling for the regular students to earn credits.

1. Broadcast Lecture Courses—Two Credit per Course

(A) Broadcast Lectures (TV, Radio and Internet): For the 2nd Semester (October 2013-March 2014) of 2013, 262 Faculty of Liberal Arts courses and 72 School of Graduate Studies courses; a total of 332 courses (refer to the Table1), are available through television and radio. Most of the television lectures and all of the radio lectures are also made available through the Internet.

These broadcast lecture courses are on principle offered for four years (two semesters per year, totaling eight semesters). Therefore, approximately one quarter of the total courses is subject to replacement each year.

Total Subjects Offered in 2013

	1st Semester		*2nd Semester*		
	TV Subjects	*Radio Subjects*	*TV Subjects*	*Radio Subjects*	*Total*
Faculty of Liberal Arts	153	109	153	109	262
School of Graduate Studies	24	46	24	46	70
Total	177	155	177	155	332

(B) *Textbooks*: Printed Materials The OUJ courses are designed to be studied through both broadcast lectures and textbooks which are specially written for each of the courses by the OUJ academic staffs and/or other experts in the given field. Some of the textbooks are highly valued by the general public and even after termination of the courses; some are revised with a fresh look and sold as the "OUJ Book Series".

2. Schooling (Face-to-Face) Courses- One Credit per Course

Classroom sessions, known as "schooling", along with broadcast lectures, are pivotal in teaching and learning at OUJ. The number of schooling offered at study centers throughout the country during the 2013 academic year was 3,110 (1st semester: 1,537, 2nd semester: 1,573). These sessions cover a wide range of subjects' characteristic to the Faculty of Liberal Arts. In addition to usual lectures and hands-on experiments, the class sessions sometimes include a variety of formats such as fieldworks and on-site observation visits.

Classroom sessions are usually designed, planned and held at the Study Centers throughout the country. The Study Centers in each locale not only offer general courses but courses in distinctive subjects unique to the given region such as history and culture, industry, nature, and so on. Furthermore, several Study Centers collaborate with nearby universities and research facilities to offer such courses.

3. Online Courses—One or Two Credits per Course

For the first time in the history of the university, full online courses are offered in 2015. Those online courses utilize the learning management system, Moodle, to deliver video lectures as well as reading materials online so that students can view those lecture videos and read related materials at anytime and anywhere. Online quizzes given at the end of each session test students' understanding of the materials and students can get immediate feedback after taking those quizzes. In addition, students can ask questions directly to the instructors and also participate in online forums to discuss materials with other students. Those courses are created by course teams that include the instructor(s), instructional designers, production crews, and a programme manager. OUJ is planning to significantly expand the line-up of online courses in coming years. Student learning activities and assessment methods in those online courses will be designed according to the objective of each course.

Broadcasting System

OUJ's facilities include the number of equipments for producing television and radio broadcast lectures. There are three TV and three radio studios where more than 1,200 broadcast lecture programmes are produced every year. OUJ's recorded TV and radio lecture programmes are broadcasted from the OUJ's transmission facilities, from early morning till late night, throughout the nation. At present, most radio lecture programmes and some TV lecture programmes are also available online as on demand video.

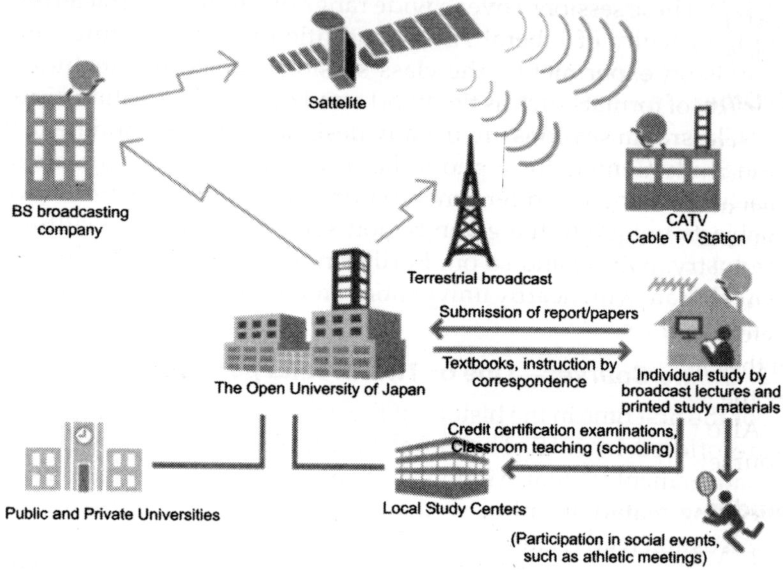

Online Services

1. Online Video-on-Demand of Broadcast Lecture Programmes

OUJ has been providing broadcast lectures online since 2007. The number of courses made available online has increased as listed.

Number of Subjects Covered by Internet Distribution in the 2013 Academic Year

	TV	*Radio*
Undergraduate	123	109
Graduate	12	46
Special Lectures	24	43
Total	159	198

2. Use of Learning Management System (LMS) Moodle

In the 2010 academic year, OUJ launched LMS using the open software, Moodle, for online exercises and student assessments.

3. "System WAKABA" and "Campus Network"

An online student administration system was put into place in the 2009 academic year. The registered students are now able to check their academic records, enroll for classes, as well as keep up to date with other sorts of matters. Since the System WAKABA enables each student to check his/her own progress, the student is now able to manage his/her own course of study.

4. Other Online Services

Web conferencing system was introduced in 2010 as part of student services offered mainly at the School of Graduate Studies. The system is called V-cube (Nice to Meet You) and used to facilitate communication between teachers and students.

OUJ became a member of the Japan Open Courseware (JOCW) in April 2010 and made some courses publicly available online in October 2010. JOCW is an associate consortium and the member of the Open Courseware Consortium (OCWC), which was started by the Massachusetts Institute of Technology in 2005.

Also OUJ opens some of the lectures for public as OUJ Open Courseware (Japanese Only).

Student Assessment

1. *Mid-Term Assignment*: After the 8th week of the broadcast lecture courses, the students are required to complete the mid-term assignment. The assignment is originally paper-based, but since the 2010 academic year, the online version has been also made available as an option to those students who wish to complete the assignment online. Completing the assignment is one of the requirements before taking the final exam at the end of the semester.

2. *Final Examination*: At the end of the 15th week of broadcast lecture courses, the students are required to sit on final exams which are carried out in their registered Study Centers. Those students who pass the exams will be granted credits.

Study Centers

OUJ has 50 Study Centers (4 in Tokyo), 7 Satellite Spaces and 70 Audio-visual Rooms throughout Japan. The Study Centers are used for conducting face-to-face class sessions and credit certification examinations. In addition, tutorials, and academic counseling are offered there. There are facilities for students to view or listen to broadcast lectures, and library services are also provided at the Study Centers. They also function as venues for students to hold extracurricular activities and friendly exchanges.

The Study Centers are located on campuses of public/private universities or in facilities of municipalities. The Satellite Spaces and Audio-visual Rooms are established for giving easier access to the above mentioned facilities to those students who live far away from the Study Centers in their prefectures.

International Cooperation

OUJ has made collaborative agreements with eleven universities worldwide, as of 2014. Under these international exchange agreements, OUJ will direct its efforts towards collaborative course material development, joint research, dual degree programmes, and exchange of faculty member, administrative staff and students, in collaboration with the partner institutions.

OUJ works in cooperation with the public and private universities. The full-time Faculty, with the help of Visiting Professors and Associate Professors and of part-time instructors, produces broadcast materials and textbooks.

Country	*University*
Canada	Athabasca University
Taiwan	National Open University
China	Shengyang Radio and TV University
Rep. of Korea	Korea National Open University
China	The Open University of China
U.S.A.	University of Maryland University College
Thailand	Sukhothai Thammathirat Open University
U.K.	The Open University
Spain*	Madrid Open University
Bhutan*	Sherubste College, Royal University of Bhutan
Spain	Universitat Oberta de Catalunya

* Universities that concluded collaborative agreement with the Center for Open Distance Education of the Open University of Japan.

The University has a great influence the improvement of education, especially higher education in Japan.

14

Open University of Malaysia

In Malaysia the provision for education is the biggest challenge for the government as the nation strives to become a fully developed country by the year 2020. One solution is to use technology as an enabler to bring education to the masses. University are taking up the challenge by updating the content of their programmes but more importantly, utilizing the latest technologies to improve delivery systems. One of the emerging delivery systems much talked about is Open and Distance Education which is fast becoming the way of providing education to the masses. As a result of this new phenomenon, in August 1999 the Ministry of Education invited Multimedia Technology Enhancement Operation Sdn, Bhd,(METEOR), a consortium of 11 public universities in the country, to set up an open university. The more by the Minister led to the establishment of Open University of Malaysia (OUM) in August 2002 followed by its official launching on 26 August 2002 by the then Prime Minister of Malaysia YAB Dato Seri Dr. Mahathir Mohamad.

The Open University of Malaysia (OUM) is the seventh private university in Malaysia. Although incorporated as a private university under the Private Higher Education Institutions Act 1996, the university leverages on the quality, prestige and capabilities of its strategic partners -a consortium of the 11 public universities. OUM adopts the motto "university for All" which is consistent with its philosophy on democratization of education. The philosophy underlies the belief that education should be made available to all, regardless of time, place, age and social economic background. The open and distance learning (ODL) mode is specifically targeted at working adult who need to take care of their families as well as manage their careers while pursuing higher education. Under the able stewardship of the then founder and

President/vice Chancellor, the late Tan Sri Dr. Abdullah Sanusi Ahmad, OUM has positional itself as an alternative avenue for the public to gain quality tertiary and lifelong education. As an open learning institution, OUM subscribe to the following principles:

- Flexible entry requirements to provide more opportunities for the members of the society to pursue their aspirations;
- A student-friendly academic system where the constraints and needs of working adults are well understood;
- A learning mode that incorporates learner's interaction with lecturers, online learning and self study, thus enriching learning experiences.

OUM's strengths span a wide range of disciplines from IT and Engineering to the Arts and Social Sciences. Business and Science. Employing the latest approaches in the teaching-learning process, it offers academic programmes that cater to the demands of industry and the marketplace in general. Initially opening its doors to 753 learners in 201, OUM, has over 79,000 students in 70 academic programmes in its eighth year operations, a record of some sort. Though OUM, working adult can upgrade their knowledge and skills for the purpose of career progression, or pursuing lifelong long learning ambition, all within the comfort of their homes.

Faculties

- Faculties of Business and Management (OUM Business School)
- Faculty of Education and Languages
- Faculties of Applied and Social Science
- Faculties of Information Technology and Multimedia Communication
- Faculties of Science and Technology
- Center for Graduate Studies

Academic Support Centers

- Center for Instructional Design and Technology
- Institute of Quality, Research and Innovation
- Center for Student Management
- Learner Service Center
- Institute for Teaching and Learning Advancement

Schools and Courses

- School of Science and Technology
- School of Health Science

Postgraduate Programmes

Center for Graduate Studies

The Center for Graduate studies (CGS) aims to provide quality postgraduate programmes in the open and distance learning environment through multi-mode learning methods. It is the nerve center for post graduate studies in OUM. It plans, manages and coordinates all postgraduate programmes at the University, working in concert with the subject matter expects, facilitators, moderators, supervisors, examiners and other professionals.

The objects of the Center are to:

- Provide postgraduate education across the disciplines
- Act as a focal point for all matters relating to postgraduate studies
- Promote the enhance a new body of knowledge by integrating multidisciplinary fields of study
- Promote research and development in relevant areas of academic interest
- Promote and enhance lifelong learning in postgraduate programmes through state-of-the-art technology and multi-mode learning delivery

The major functions of the Center are to:

- Plan manage coordinate and facilitate postgraduate programmes locally and internationally
- Implement and review rules and regulations for postgraduate studies including curriculum, research requirements and other academic matters
- Assist the various faculties in planning implementing and ensuring quality postgraduate programmes
- Provide management support for postgraduate learners and academic staff
- Promote collaborations with local and international institutions

Currently, CGS manages the following programmes:

Master's Degree

- Master of Human Resource Management
- Master of Project Management
- Master of Instructional design and Technology
- Master of Software Engineering
- Master of Sciences (Business Administration)
- Master of Environmental Science
- Master of Education
- Master of Information Science (Competitive Intelligence)
- Master of Business Administration
- Master of Managements
- Master of Information Technology
- Master of Multimedia Communication
- Master of Environmental Science

PhD Degrees

- Doctor of philosophy (Business Administration)
- Doctor of philosophy (Engineering)
- Doctor of philosophy (Information Technology)
- Doctor of philosophy (Science)
- Doctor of philosophy (Education)

Technologies in Use

Asynchronous Communication

- E-mail
- Microblogging (e.g. Twitter)
- Online Forms/Threaded discussions
- Podcasts
- RSS feeds
- SMS/MMS
- Social Networking Utilities (e.g. Face book, MySpace)
- Voicemail

Synchronous Communication

- Instant Messaging (e.g. ICQ, MSN)
- Online Forms (e.g. Eluminate)
- Teleconferencing
- Telephone
- Video Conferencing

Blended Learning Methodology

- Face-to-learning: Tutorials were conducted where students have the opportunity to physically meet their tutors and discussed their subject and their assignment.
- e-Learning: Students are required to participate in an online forum using a learning management system and discussed among each other's and with their tutors and peers on their subject matters and on their assignment.
- Self-managed learning module: Students do not have to come over for their tutorials but they still need to come for their tests. They learn by using participating in the learning management system and using their own modules.
- M-Learning: The learning materials are designed in downloadable formats that can be accessed using a desktop or laptop computer. Students then opt to transfer these contents into a handphone to view them. One needs a handphone equipped with the necessary features.

OUM has a strong network of learning centers nationwide. These learning centers are in major cities and towns, from Peninsular Malaysia to Sabah and Sarawak. OUM has 53 learning centers fully equipped with tutorial rooms, computer laboratories, library and Internet facilities.

- Modules are used by the students, tutors and subject matter experts (SEMs). The modules are written by academicians from public and private universities in Malaysia
- The Tan Sri Dr. Abdullah Sanusi Digital library has more than 30,000 volumes of printed books in the main campus and learning centers nationwide. As for the digital collection, the online databases consist of more than 82,000 e-books and 32,000 e-journal titles. Other electronics collections include electronic theses, newspaper articles and legal acts.
- iRadio OUM is Malaysia's first internet radio station to base its segment on modules offered by a university. iRadio OUM was established in April 2007. Boasting shows mainly aimed to add value to OUM learner's open and distance education, iRadio OUM is the creativity link, bridging education and information with entertainment in hopes to provide an alternative outlet for those looking for entertainment and education in the World Wide Web.

Summary of External Quality Assurance Processes

OUM is legally established and all programmes are accredited by Malaysian Qualification Agency (MQA). A few departments are certified with MS ISO 9001; 2008

- In Malaysia the national quality assurance or accreditation framework for higher education is under the purview of the MQA a statutory body established under the Malaysian Qualification Agency Act 2007 to accredit academic programmes provided post secondary or higher education and facilitate the recognitions and articulation of qualifications. It is an independent autonomous body with a mandate to access the quality of all faces of tertiary level institutions including universities. The MQA was formally known as the National Accreditation Board (LAN), establishment under the Lembaga Akreditas Negara Act 1996 prior to its merger with the Quality Assurance Division, Ministry of Higher Education in December 2005.
- The MQA administers the Malaysian Qualification Framework (MQF) which is a unified system of post secondary qualification offered on a national basis in Malaysia.

Summary of Quality Procedures

The following are examples of QA processes adopted by the University:

- New programmes development is based on market demand and international benchmarks;
- Periodic programme review based on internal self-review, inputs from external examiners' or Board of Studies;
- Obtaining learners' and tutors' feedback;
- Consultation with relevant industry or professional bodies;
- Quarterly Management Reporting;
- Conduct internal audits and participation in external audits such as International Standards Organization (ISO), Academic Performance Audit;
- Participation in external Surveys.

15

Open Universiteit Netherland

The Open Universiteit Netherland was founded in 1984, welcoming its first students in September 1984; it is an independent government-funded institute. The administration is based in Heerlen, in the province of Limburg in the very south of the Netherland. Dispersed over the Netherlands, the Open Universiteit has 12 study centers and 3 support centers, as well as 6 study centers in Dutch-speaking Flanders (Belgium) and 1 study center in the Netherlands Antilles.

Aims

The Dutch governament's purpose in founding the Open Universiteit Netherland was to make higher education accessible to anyone with the necessary aptitudes and interests, regardless of formal qualification.

The Open Universiteit identifies four aims:

- to create a cost-effective form of higher education,
- to encourage innovation in Dutch higher education, in terms of both curriculum and teaching methods,
- to reduce the teacher shortage in Dutch primary and secondary schools, and
- to be a recognized player in (commercial) distance and e-learning training programmes and consultancy.

Departments and Faculties

The Open Universiteit consists of seven faculties:

- School of Management,
- School of Cultural studies,
- School of Informatics,
- School of Natural Sciences,

- School of Psychology,
- School of Law,
- School of Education

Each faculty is headed by a dean of studies, who supervises teams of subject specialists and educational technologists engage in developing courses and programmes, often in co-operation with specialists from other universities or from trade and industry.

In addition to this, the university has two expertise centers: The Centre for Learning Sciences and Technologies (CELSTEC), which develops innovative teaching methods for distance education and higher education in general, and the Ruud the Moor Centre, which seeks to support professionals in secondary education. CELSTEC consist of three Research and Development programmes covering the topics of Learning and Cognition, Learning Networks for Professional Development, and Learning Media. The School of Education staff are all CELSTEC staff members. CELSTECs Research and Development work is also aimed to support the Schools of the Open Universiteit.

Furthermore, the Open universiteit has two support staff departments. They are the department of Business Services and the department of Support Services. Together they provide operational services, ranging from student administration to the distribution of course materials

Study Programmes

The Open Universiteit offers three types of study programmes:

1. Bachelor and Master degree programmes. The Open Universiteit offers fully accredited Bachelor or Master degree programmes in Law, Economics, Business and Public administration, Engineering, Environmental science, Cultural studies, Psychology and Education. The university converted its programmes to the Bachelors-Master structure in September 2002.
2. Short programmes. Students can also follow short programmes. These include short vocational training courses, postgraduate courses and short undergraduate programmes, which are developed in co-operation with universities of professional education, academic universities, professional bodies or commercial companies.
3. Courses Besides these academic programmes, students can

choose from over 300 modular courses. This modular course system implies that student can enrol either for full-length degree programmes or choose to study one of over 400 individual courses.

Most course-material is in Dutch, but more and more material is becoming available in English. Examinations are in general in Dutch and have to be taken at one of the locations of the Open Universiteit, that is, ether at a study center or at a support centers in the Netherlands, Flanders or the Netherlands Antilles. For individuals there are possibilities to have (under stric supervision conditions) an exam taken at an alternative location, such as Dutch embassies, in prisons or on a ship.

Students

People from all walks of life and all ages take advantage of the Open Universiteit. There are no entry requirements other than the ability to study at an appropriate level. The Open universiteit is especially popular with those who cannot physically attend a traditional university (because they are disabled, aboard, in prison, or serving in the armed forces), or who wish to study a first (or additional) degree while holding down a full-time job, whether to progress their career or allow them to change their career. About 70 per cent of the students remain in paid employment throughout their studies.

Study Centers

Netherlands

- Alkmaar
- Amsterdam
- Breda
- The Hague
- Eindhoven (at the Eindhoven University of Technology)
- Emmen, support center
- Enschede
- Groningen
- Heerlen, also main office
- Leeuwarden, support center
- Nijmegen (at the Radboud University Nijmegen)
- Rotterdam
- Utrecht
- Vlissingen, support center
- Zwolle

Belgium (Flanders)

- Antwerp (at the university of Antwerp)
- Brussels (at vrije universiteit Brussels)
- Diepenbeek (at limburgs Universitair Centrum)
- Ghent (at Ugent)
- Kortrijk (at KU leuven-kortrijk)
- Leuven (at KU Leuven)

16

Open University of Sri Lanka

Open University of Sri Lanka (OUSL) is a national university in Sri Lanka. It is unique within the Sri Lankan national university system for being the only university to offer programmes of study leading to Certificate, Diploma, Degrees and Postgraduate degrees up to PhD level through the Distance Mode Learning. The degrees awarded by the university are treated as equivalent to degrees awarded by any other Sri Lankan University under the preview of the University Grants Commission.

Establishment

The concept of establishing the Open University of Sri Lanka was by Dr. Nissanka Wijeyeratne the Cabinet Minister of Education and Higher Education at the time.

The University was set up by the Government of Sri Lanka under the Universities Act No. 16 of 1978, for the purpose of providing higher educational opportunities to working adults—providing them the road to success, surpassing age, vocation, gender, race, ethnicity and religion. The OUSL has the same legal and academic status as any other national university in Sri Lanka.

The university policy on admission would enable a person to register at the lowest 'Level' with mere basic literacy and then climb up to postgraduate level.

The concept of Distance Education at the OUSL functions through a dynamic network of regional and study centres, with knowledge imparted through multiple media. Therefore, students with work commitments are able to pursue studies since they interact with especially designed self-instructional materials where the materials function as a "Tutor in Print". This method provides the distance learner with the best possible learning opportunity to enable a balancing of personal, work related and academic obligations.

Vision

"To be the premier Open and Distance Learning institution in Asia through excellence, efficiency and equity in Lifelong Learning."

Mission

"To enhance access to high quality, affordable and relevant education through Open Distance Education and ensure life-long learning opportunities to face challenges in a knowledge society."

Management Structure

The authorities are:

1. The Council 2. The Senate 3. The Faculty Board

The Council of the University is the executive and academic body and the governing authority of the University.

The Senate is the academic authority of the University. The University had initially the following Faculties:

1. Faculty of Engineering and Technology
2. Faculty of Natural Sciences
3. Faculty of Humanities and Social Sciences

The academic and administrative head of each Faculty is the Dean.

OUSL Regional Centers and Study Centers

OUSL Regional Centers

Location	*Officer in-Charge*
Colombo	Assistant Director
Anuradhapura	Assistant Director
Baticaloa	Snr. Assistant Director
Jaffna	Assistant Director
Kandy	Assistant Director
Matara	Assistant Director

Study Centers

- Ambalantota
- Ampara
- Badulla
- Bandarawela
- Galle
- Hatton
- Kalutara
- Kegalle

- Killinochchi
- Kurunegala
- Monaragala
- Polonnaruwa
- Puttalam
- Ratnapura
- Trincomalee
- Vaunia

Faculties

The University consists of five Faculties and one postgraduate institute and several divisions. The Faculties are:

1. Faculty of Education
2. Faculty of Engineering Technology
3. Faculty of Humanities and Social Sciences
4. Faculty of Natural Sciences
5. Faculty of Health Sciences
6. Postgraduate Institute of English (PGIE)

Faculty of Education

The Faculty of Education was established in 2003 and currently consists of three departments. These three departments are:

1. Department of Secondary and Tertiary Education
2. Department of Early Childhood and Primary Education
3. Department of Special Needs Education

Faculty of Engineering Technology

The Faculty of Engineering Technology of OUSL offers Bachelor of Technology Honours in Engineering [BTech Eng (Hons)], Bachelor of Industrial studies (BIS) and Bachelor of Software Engineering (BSE). Bachelor of Technology Honours in Engineering degree offered by the Faculty of Engineering Technology is highly recognised by professional Engineering Institution (IESL); both local and overseas to work as qualified Graduate Engineers. It is also the pioneers of introducing Mechatronics Engineering to Sri Lankan engineering education curricula and would be proud of producing first graduate engineers in Mechatronics engineering on 2010 in Sri Lanka. The Faculty consists of six departments. These six departments are:

1. Department of Agricultural and Plantation Engineering
2. Department of Electrical and Computer Engineering
3. Department of Mechanical Engineering
4. Department of Textile and Apparel Technology

5. Department of Civil Engineering
6. Department of Mathematics and Philosophy of Engineering

Faculty also offers two Master of Technology programmes in Industrial Engineering and Construction management; each conduct by Mechanical Engineering and Civil Engineering departments respectively.

Faculty of Humanities and Social Sciences

The Faculty of Humanities and Social Sciences (HSS) is the largest faculty of the OUSL. The Faculty consists of the four following departments:

1. Department of Language Studies
2. Department of Law
3. Department of Social Studies
4. Department of Management

Faculty of Natural Sciences

The Faculty of Natural Sciences was established in 1987[8] and consists of the six following departments:

1. Department of Botany
2. Department of Chemistry
3. Department of Mathematics and Computer Science
4. Department of Physics
5. Department of Zoology

Faculty of Health Sciences

The Faculty of Health Sciences is the youngest faculty of the university and established in August 2015. And consists of six academic departments.

1. Department of Basic Sciences
2. Department of Health Education and Research
3. Department of Pharmacy,
4. Department of Nursing,
5. Department of Medical Laboratory Sciences
6. Department of Psychology and Counselling

Non-Academic/Support Divisions

- Library Services

- Educational Technology
- Regional Educational Services
- Information Technology
- Staff Development Centre

Administrative Divisions

The administration is done by other Divisions:

- Finance Division
- Information Technology Division
- Establishment Division
- General Administration Division
- Student Affairs Division
- Regional Educational Services Division
- Public Information office
- Maintenance Division
- Operations Division
- Internal and Government Audit Division

Study Centers of OUSL

There are 17 study centers in OUSL distributed all over Sri Lanka.

1. Ambalangoda (M041) - 80/1. Polwatte Road, Halwatura, Ambalangoda
2. Ambalantota (M051) - Rajasaranagama Road, Lunama South, Ambalantota
3. Ampara (K080) - Inginiyagala Road, Samapura, Ampara
4. Badulla (U 190) - Advanced Technical IUnstitute, Badulla
5. Bandarawela (K120) - St Thomas Road, Wewatenna, Bandarawela
6. Galle (M040) - Labuduwa, Galle
7. Gampaha (C200) - Gampaha Road, Miriswatte, Mudungoda
8. Hatton (K122) - Thomndaman Vocational Training Center, Hatton
9. Kegalle (K140) - Kumarathunga Munidasa Mawatha, Kegalle
10. Kalutara (C020) - 66/2, Nagoda Road, Kalutara
11. Kurunegala (K190) - Negambo Rd, Nissanka mawatha Junction, Kurunegala
12. Moneragala (M180) - Technical College Junction, Sirigala, Potuvil Rd., Moneragala
13. Polonnaruwa (K150) - 24, Post Bediwewa, Jayanthipura, Polonnaruwa
14. Puttalam (C135) - 1/137, Colombo Rd., Puttalam

15. Ratnapura (C130) - Hiddellna, Ratnapura
16. Vavuniya (J160) - No. 366, Kandy Rd., Thekkawaththai, Vavuniya
17. Kilinochchi (K032) - Lwa Resources Center, Kandy Rd, Kilinochchi

Components of Learning System

1. Printed Material
2. Audio-Visual Devices
3. Demonstrations and Practical Works
4. Tutoring and Counselling
5. Assignments and Assessments

Student Enrolment

Student Enrolment by Faculty and Programme of Study, 2013

Level of Programmes		*Education*	*Engineering Technology*	*Humanities and Social Sciences*	*Natural Sciences*	*Total*
Master Degree Programmes		453	27	357	103	940
	%	48.19	2.87	37.98	10.96	100.00
Post Graduate Diploma Programmes		5364	58	25	20	5467
	%	98.12	1.06	0.45	0.37	100.00
Undergraduate Programmes		163	2093	7713	6770	16739
	%	0.97	12.50	46.08	40.45	100.00
Diploma Programmes		780	2515	367	56	3718
	%	20.98	67.64	9.87	1.51	100.00
Certificate Programmes		1908	147	6445	263	8763
	%	21.77	1.68	73.55	3.00	100.00
Foundation Programmes		—	1834	—	833	2667
	%	—	68.77	—	31.23	100.00
Total		**8668**	**6674**	**14907**	**8045**	**38294**
	%	22.64	17.43	38.92	21.01	100.00

Study Method

The distance learning methodology adopted by the OUSL may initially appear as a challenging task to students. In addition to gaining subject knowledge and skills, students develop many other life skills, including, self-organization, and time management. Regular lectures, a feature of face-to-face teaching at a conventional university, is minimal at the OUSL. Instead, students learn through with other forms of support that facilitate learning.

The OUSL adopts a multimedia system for teaching with a strong emphasis on distance learning. The study system supports the students through printed course material, audio visual aids, discussions, day schools, tutor clinics, lab and field works, industry visits, web based learning, etc. Continuous assessments and final examinations are also integral parts of the study system.

Printed course material is the center element in the study package. Improving reading skills is therefore essential to be successful as an OUSL student. Where applicable, students will also be provided with other supportive material applicable to a course, such as study guides, practical guides, audio visual material, etc. Printed course materials are carefully prepared to suit self study and independent learning. The printed course materials provide the students the subject knowledge of the course. The clearly outline the objectives of the course and what the student will be able to achieve by studying the course. Self-assessment questions and activities included in the course material will enable the learners to continuously assess themselves as they proceed. Printed course materials are normally provided at the time of registration for a programme/course.

Programme of Study: A Programme of study consists of a combination of compulsory and optional courses, which leads to a certificates, certificate of advanced study, diploma, degree or a postgraduate degree.

Stand Alone Course: A Stand Alone Course is a course which can be considered as a separate entity. These courses can be offered by any person who wishes to upgrade the knowledge in a particular subject area, without registering for a regular programme of study, such as a Degree/Certificate Programme. many courses of the Degree Programmes are offered as Stand Alone Courses.

Continuing Education Courses: Continuing education courses are offered for students registered for regular programmes of study who wish to widen their knowledge in areas of their choice These include support courses, such as Mathematics, English, Computer literacy, etc. A student can offer a limited number of continuing education courses, over and above the maximum workload allowed during an academic year.

Foundation Courses in Science: Foundation Courses in Science are courses offered for those who lack academic qualifications equivalent to that of G.C.E. Advanced Level in Sri Lanka. Thus, these are particularly suited for students who lack direct entry requirements for the Degree Programme.

Credit Rating

Programmes as well as courses carry a credit rating. The 'Credit Rating' is the expression used in the OUSL to denote the "Academic value" of a course/programme. Please note that the word credit does not imply any measure of academic performance at an examination such as Credit Pass at G.C.E O/L or A/L Examination. The Credit rating gives a measure of the time expected to be spent on studying the course. At the OUSL, one credit is about 45 hours of study time. The time specified for a course involved, including reading and understanding course material, face-to-face sessions, continuous assessments, final examinations, consultation of reference materials, practical classes, etc.

Support for Learning

Each student is assigned a personal tutor/counselor during the pre-registration orientation sessions of some programmes. The Personal Tutor will guide the students and provide greater awareness about the university, the study system and other particulars regarding the programme of study.

Students are also reminded that it is mandatory to get the registration forms certified by the Personal Tutor before coming for registration.

Day Schools

Day Schools are interactive sessions where the student will get the opportunity to meet the respective course teachers to clarify any difficulty they come across in their study material. Attendance at day schools is not compulsory. However, attending a day school well prepared will immensely help students perform well in the courses. Day schools are held almost at all Regional Centers and the students have the option of attending a Day school held at a center of their choice.

Tutor clinics are normally held just before the end of semester final exams as an additional help for students preparing for final exams.

Online Support and MyOUSL

In order to give the students additional help and also to familiarize them with modern learning trends and tools, some courses are supplemented with an online component. The online activities could be accessed from home or from the National Online Distance Education Service Access Centers (NAC centers) located at centers specified in Regional centers. Once the student register for a course with an online component, student will be further advised on how to access and use it.

Through MyOUSL, the link, students may access online moodle courses, personal details, timetables, payment details, submit final exam applications, etc.

Teaching/Learning Method

The central element of the self-study is the printed material that offers the student the equivalent of lectures in a conventional university. They also provide a series of carefully designed activities and self-assessment questions, which help the student to develop analytical skills and independent thought. Printed material are supported by, audio-visual material, day schools (face to face discussions), tutor clinics, laboratory work, fieldwork, on-line component and seminars.

Laboratory work and field work form an integral part of most courses in technology and are compulsory.

Pre-scheduled day schools and tutor clinics are conducted by the academics of the Faculty for groups of students at Regional and Study Centres of the University. In these day schools, students can discuss difficulties that they have encountered in the self-study materials of a particular course.

The OUSL is meant primarily for working students. Therefore, it should be possible for a student to study while working, without much difficulty. While the University is making every effort to schedule as many activities as possible during weekends and public holidays, certain activities such as laboratory classes and examinations may have to be scheduled during weekdays. Since the activity schedule for the whole year is given to the students at the beginning of the academic year, it is hoped that they can plan their work well in advance.

Consultancies and Services

The OUSL is the most outreached academic institution in Sri Lanka with 6 regional centres, 19 study centres and 6 teaching centres distributed throughout the island. The OUSL consists of four academic faculties namely, Engineering Technology, Natural Sciences, Education and Humanities and Social Sciences. Also OUSL consists of divisions such as, Centre for Educational Technology and Media (CETMe), Staff Development Centre (SDC), Career Guidance Unit, Information Technology Division (IT) and printing press. These faculties and divisions consist of well qualified academics, technical and other staff members and physical resources such as modern state of the art laboratory, sophisticated equipment, studio and recording facilities, modern printing machinery, etc.

The Consultancy and External Recourses Centre (CERC) is a division established by the Open University of Sri Lanka (OUSL) in order to facilitate and enhance the collaboration between the University and the Sri Lankan community. Also through CERC the university can utilize its human and physical resources, when available, to the betterment of the country. The CERC is managed by a Board of Management comprising the Vice-Chancellor who is the chairman of the board, director and nominated member of both academic and administrative staff.

The CERC undertakes assignments such as research programmes, consultancy services, extension courses, training and continuing professional development courses. The academics of respective academic departments and divisions could undertake such assignments without prejudice to the primary commitments to the OUSL. Some of the CERC assignments are developed by the academic department after analyzing the current trends and needs of the society. Also there are many assignments which are tailor made to suit the requirement of the client who is an external institution. A CERC project can commence, once the approval has been granted by the chairman of CERC. The OUSL will offer the required physical and human resources to conduct and complete the assignment successfully.

Centre for Educational Technology and Media (CETMe)

The Centre for Educational Technology and Media (CETMe) plays a pivotal role in the Open University of Sri Lanka (OUSL) in providing guidelines for designing self-instructional materials, designing and developing educational media and ensuring quality standards of the OUSL course materials. It is the service provider for all the four faculties to develop their courses including online courses.

So far the centre has won 9 international awards for educational videos from Japan, Iran and UNDP.

The CETMe consists of two main units; Academic and Research Unit and Production Unit (Media House).

Academic and Research Unit

The Academic and Research Unit is responsible for the following:

- formulating guidelines and mechanisms for course design and development (print, audio-visual and online)
- conducting capacity building workshops for academic staff of the OUSL in writing self-instructional materials, designing and developing audio-visual and online courses
- facilitating and assisting the development of course material (print, audio-visual and online)
- administering and uploading of all online courses
- copyediting of OUSL course materials and other OUSL publications
- ensuring quality standards of the OUSL course material and
- carrying out Open and Distance Learning (ODL) research

Innovation Grants

Open University of Sri Lanka seeks to promote innovations and would like to help the academic staff and the students (both graduate and postgraduate) pursuing innovations. There is a strong emphasis on innovative solutions to address unique and complex challenges of the 21st century. In this regard, the key question would be "How do we find resources and support to begin such innovative projects?"

As the first step in answering the question above, the OUSL Innovation Grants programme is being initiated to support innovations, explorations, and other scientific developments by way of designs, products and methods etc in order to raise awareness and encourage engagement in innovative efforts by the members of the academic staff and the students of the OUSL. Grant recipients receive a maximum of Rs. 100,000/- as financial support for such work.

These Innovation Grants are open to members of the academic staff and current students of the Open University of Sri Lanka. You may obtain matching grants in cash or thing (e.g. resources from collaborators) in order to complete the innovation project with the prior approval of the OUSL. In providing funds, the specified project goals, the feasibility of optimum utilization of the outcome of the innovation and long-term sustainability etc may become important factors.

Environmental Studies Unit

The Centre for Environmental Studies and Sustainable Development (CESSD) of the Open University of Sri Lanka (OUSL) was established in 1998 having the primary aim of educating the environmental officers of the Central Environmental Authority (CEA) and the Ministry of Environment by offering Post Graduate Diploma in Environmental Science. Since 2007 the CESSD offers the Master of Science degree Programme in Environmental Sciences which is designed and conducted by a team of outside experts and academics of faculties at the Open University, viz: Natural Sciences, Engineering Technology, Education and Humanities and Social Sciences.

The Master's Degree is designed to provide students with the interdisciplinary background and skills necessary to understand the environmental issues prevailing today. It emphasizes four general areas; humanities and social sciences, technology, education and natural sciences. Humanities and social sciences emphasizes the ethical, legal, economical, political and historical basis of the environmental concern. The Natural science focus includes the exploitation of the biological, physical, chemical nature of the environment and Technology deals with problem creations and problem solutions. Further the CESSD is addressing Environmental Pollution, Biodiversity Loss, Wildlife Conservation, Deforestation, Sustainable Development, Climate Change, Environmental Impact Assessments and Environmental Policies through researches, collaborative works with other agencies and events in the environmental arena.

Research

The key mandate of universities world over is mainly teaching and research. However, this mandate has been relegated in many universities in Sri Lanka. High quality university education involving training and research not only provides the human capital for socio economic development but also transforms individuals and societies through poverty reduction and increased global competitiveness.

The Open University of Sri Lanka (OUSL) recognizes that developing the capacity of its academic staff by providing them with opportunities to engage in research would pave path to explore and validate novel ideas in research, innovation and other intellectual activities. This would, in turn, contribute to national development in the long term. Thus, on the initiative and recommendation of the Vice Chancellor, the OUSL established the Research Division in February 2014 to serve as a vehicle to spearhead its research mandate. This Division is headed by the Director, Research.

The OUSL with the support of its Research Division will bring together research and education across a broad spectrum of science, engineering, social science, management and other areas in order to foster multidisciplinary discoveries and inventions that arise through the mixing of students, faculty and researchers across traditional disciplinary boundaries.

The Open University of Sri Lanka seeks to conduct and promote high quality multidisciplinary research to develop the capacity of the academics and also to help policy makers in Sri Lanka. To this end, the OUSL welcomes multidisciplinary research proposals from academic community of OUSL in a wide range of disciplines and professional fields that address issues related to its research priority areas in the field of both natural and social sciences.

The Official Policy State of the University on Distance Education Research is:

> The OUSL is committed to undertake continuing research on distance education to achieve its mission of increasing access to and success in adult learning at University level and to enhance the quality of equal opportunities for adult Sri Lankans. Distance Education Research is an indispensable tool in OUSL's efforts towards excellence in teaching and scholarship while ensuring social equity.

To facilitate research by staff, the staffs undertaking research are released for 50 percent of time for a period of 3 months. Resources needed for such research provided from the University Research Fund. Distance Education Research/Publications are given explicit recognition in schemes of recruitment up to a maximum of 50 percent of the requirement. OUSL Journal enables findings of distance education research to be disseminated workshops are conducted to develop research skills in academic and academic support staff. Research surveys are conducted on OUSL graduates, OUSL support system, quality of studying material, quality of contact sessions and student participation. Evaluations of several programmes of study are also concerned.

Despite policy decisions taken in release of academics for research, very few faculty members have requested to be released from the normal work to undertake research. Moreover an external constraint imposed by the freezing of cadre positions by UGC has added to the workload of academic staff, thus having an adverse impact on research. Despite constraints, promise of greater involvement of staff in distance education research is indicated.

17

Open University of United Kingdom

The Open University, established in the United Kingdom by Royal Charter in 1969, was the first distance teaching university that was truly multimedia in nature. It was rapidly adapted in other countries and various accounts were written about its history. *The Open University Opens* by Jeremy Tuntstall (1974), The Open *University from Within* by John Ferguson (1975), *Open University* by Walter Perry (1976), *How Open is Open?* by A. Woodley (1979), *The Open University: A History* by Daniel Weinbren (2015) are some of the accounts of the Open University.

In 1964, Harold Wilson, the new Prime Minister asked Jennie Lee, a junior minister in the Department of Education and Science, to take special responsibility for the University of the Air project. Committed to the establishment of a University with high academic standards, she gained Government Commitment to the project. In 1967 the Government established a Planning Committee. The Planning Committee Report was published in 1969, providing a blue-print for the University. A Royal Charter was granted in June 1969, establishing the Open University as an independent and autonomous institution authorized to confer its own degrees.

Major Problems Encountered in Establishing the University

Watter Perry, the first Vice-Chancellor highlighted 7 such problems:

1. Political problems
2. What sort of university should it be?
3. Finding students
4. Educational problems
5. Social problems
6. Administrative problems
7. Financial problems

Formal Governance Structure

The OU was established by Royal Charter on 23 April 1969. Two statutory bodies of the Universities are the Council and the Senate.

The University's main governing body is the Council, supported by a number of sub-committees. Council has a membership of 25 and includes representative of academic and research staff, associate lecture and non-academic staff, students, and a number of external co-opted members. These external members, appointed for their experience and expertise, hold the majority of Council places.

The Council is a particularly concerned with finances, property and staff. It has ultimate authority within the OU, but must respect the views of the Senate in academic matters.

The Senate is the academic authority of the University, responsible for promoting the academic work of the University, both in teaching and research. Subject to the powers of the Council, it oversees academic management, including curriculum and all aspects of quality and standards associated with the University as a degree-awarding body. Senate meetings concentrate on major issues of academic strategy, policy, priority and performance.

Organisation

The executive head of the University is the Vice-Chancellor, who is assisted by Pro-Vice-Chancellors, each with responsibility for a specified policy area. Organisationally the University is divided into five major areas:

1. The six Faculties.
2. The Center for Continuing Education
3. The Institute of Educational Technology
4. Regional Academic Services
5. Operations, responsible for course products and distribution
6. The Administration

Faculties

At the heart of the OU's teaching are its faculties, schools and institutes, producing high quality courses under pinned by research of international excellence:

1. Faculty of Arts

2. Open University Business School
3. Faculty of Education and Language Studies
4. Faculty of Health and Social Care
5. Open University Law School
6. Faculty of Mathematics, Computing and Teaching
7. Faculty of Science
8. Faculty of Social Science
9. Institute of Educational Technology
10. Knowledge Media Institute
11. Centre for Inclusion and Collaborative Partnerships

Interdisciplinary Research Centers

1. Center for Citizenship, Identification and Governance.
2. Center for Research in Education and Educational Technology
3. Research Center for Physical and Environment Sciences
4. Open Space Research Center
5. Centre for Research in Computing

Academic Programmes

The University offers several ways to study. The undergraduate programme covers a series of courses taken over a period of years leading to a degree. The continuing education programme has a very wide range of single courses and different levels, some leading to diplomas and certificates and works closely with users in-house training programme. The higher degree programme provides opportunities for both taught and research-based postgraduate study.

Undergraduates have a wide choice of courses, spanning the Arts, Social Sciences, Mathematics, Science, Technology and Educational Studies.

Undergraduate Courses are offered at four different levels-foundations, second, third and fourth. All students have to take a foundation course, which assumes no previous knowledge of the subject and provides a broad introduction to a range of subjects and study skills. After that, they can choose courses at any level though they are encouraged to progress sensibly to the more demanding higher level courses.

The printed word still remains the most accessible and easily used means of communication. Multi-media support to correspondence texts comes in the form of television and radio broadcasts and audio and video cassettes. These are an integral part of most courses. For many science and technology subjects, they are essential.

Students also have access to locally based personal tuition at study centers spread throughout the country; they also can contact their part-time tutor on telephone. Study centers are run by University's regional network.

The University uses a combination of continuous assessment and end of year examinations.

Continuing Education Programme

The scope of the University's involvement in continuing education has grown year by year. It is divided into six sectors of activity:

1. The Open Business School
2. Scientific and Technological Updating
3. Health and Social Welfare
4. Professional Development in Education
5. Community Education
6. Personal and Cultural Education

Research and Higher Degree Programme

Like other Universities, the Open University given importance to research and higher degree studies. The University offers both full-time and part-time opportunities for research based higher degrees and is now developing a number of taught higher degrees.

Students

A diverse range of students from all walks of life are attracted to the OU, for most modules there are no entry requirements other than the ability to study at an appropriate level, though most postgraduate modules require evidence of previous study or equivalent life experience. This fundamental open admissions policy makes undergraduate university study accessible to all: In 2009-10 academic year over 70 per cent students were in full-time or part-time employment, often working towards a first (or additional) degree or qualification to progress or change their career. Over 50,000 students are sponsored by their employers. The University is also popular with those who cannot physically attend a traditional university study courses because they have health limitations, are working or resident overseas, in prison, serving in the armed forces caring for family members or otherwise unable to attend or commit to traditional full-time or on-campus university study. Students are represented by the University Students Union (OUSA).

In 2009-10 academic years, there were 253,075 enrolled students, plus an additional 2,273 customers who bought courses materials but did not enroll on a course to receive academic credits. The majority of students in 2009-10 academic year were aged between 25-44 years old, with the median age of new undergraduates being 31. Most students were from England (166,936) while 15,744 were from Scotland, 8,443 from Wales, 4,255 from Northern Ireland and 12,127 fro, elsewhere in the European Union, plus others elsewhere. 61 per cent of undergraduates were female with even number among those taking postgraduate modules.

The OUs International Development Office

The Open University undertakes developments work worldwide—from programmes taught directly to projects delivered through local partners.

Programmes include:

- **HEAT**, a healthcare education and training programme transforming the skills of frontline healthcare workers across sub-Suharan Africa
- **English in Action in Bangladesh,** a technology- enhanced English language education programme on target to reach 25 million people across the country by 2017.
- **TESSA** transforming the education of primary and secondary school teachers across Sub-Saharan Africa.
- **Transforming English Language Skill in Higher Education in Pakistan** developing the use of the English language within higher education institutions in Pakistan.

The Open University in Europe and Worldwide

The Open University is the world's leading provider of flexible, high quality online degrees and distance learning, serving students across the globe with highly respected degree qualifications, including the triple-accredited MBA degree.

Open Access to Learning Materials

Every day, millions of people access free OU content, no matter where they live in the world. All they need is an internet connection:

Platform	Description
Open Learn	Free OU course materials and other educational resources, delivered through a multi-winning website. Visitors don't need to register as students.
YouTube	Over 800 videos including clips about student life, current research and extracts from OU broadcasts and teaching materials.
iTunes U	A huge range of podcasts to listen to on the move. In April 2012 OU became the first university in Europe to reach more than 1 million subscriptions.
Open Research Online	One of the largest university research collections in the UK, with more than 15,000 research publications available online.

Institute of Educational Technology (IET)

IET sets at the heart of the OU's pedagogy and research strategy, sporting the OU as a visionary leader of educational technology. This is done by exploring and understanding what is possible trying out new ideas, reflecting on what happens and why, then apply this learning to enhance the OU's teaching and helps its students IET champions open approaches to research, join with world class researchers and link research and practice; IET's work is collaborative with colleagues within the University and around the world: IET staff members help drive knowledge sharing and provide innovative leadership of educational technology for the university

IET offers postgraduate qualifications in online teaching and learning pathways on a part-time and full-time basis. Its postgraduate qualifications and modules are designed to suit new and experienced professionals who want to improve their competences or career prospects in the areas of Teaching and Learning in Higher Education, Online and Distance Learning and Educational Technology.

Quality Assurance

The innovative nature of the OU meant that from the start, it had to give a lot of attention for the quality of the education it provided if it was to achieve comparable recognition to other Universities. The public nature of its education as well as its published course materials available to the general public in virtually all books shops, its films and audio materials is broadcast on BBC television and radio meant that its quality was subject to wide public scrutiny in ways and to an extent unknown in conventional universities

The approach is quality in the OU vested importance in two things: people and systems. The innovative nature and ideology of the University attracted academic staffs who were committed

Media development and learning at the OU

1970s		1980s		1990s		2000s	
Broadcasts Of module-related television	Interactive print media	Broadcasts of module-related television	Interactive video-cassettes	Non-course-related television (outreach)	Interactive video-cassette	Non-course-related television (outreach)	Audio-visual digital media
						Mobile technology	
Broadcasts of module-related radio	Tutors • Face-to-face tutorials • Telephone tutorials • Postal correspondence • Residential schools	Broadcasts of module-related radio	Interactive audio-cassette	Interactive integrated multi-media	Interactive audio-cassette	Social media	Web 2.0 and beyond
		Interactive print media	Support media • Conferencing • email	Print media	Support media • Conferencing • email	Support media • conferencing • email	Virtual worlds
		Interactive integrated multi-media	Tutors • face-to-face tutorials • telephone tutorials • postal correspondence • residential schools	Internet Web 1.0	Tutors • face-to-face tutorials • telephone tutorials • postal correspondence • residential schools	Tutors • face-to-face tutorials • telephone tutorials • postal correspondence • residential schools	Print media

This representation of the journey from reliance on broadcast, personal and postal delivery towards and increased use of disk-based media and online delivery is based on Josie Taylor, 'Learning Journeys: the road from informal to formal learning - The UK Open University's approach' , Journal of Interactive Education, Autumn, 2013.

to teaching much as research. The OU's teaching methods attracted and rewarded talented and committed teachers.

In addition to the special quality assurance arrangements within the University, the OU also operated the quality system common to the rest of the UK higher Education. In addition, the OU courses were subject to the same professional body accreditation procedures as existed for university courses elsewhere.

In 1995 the Pro Vice-Chancellor for Quality Assurance and Research established the Quality Assurance fund to support small projects which would lead to the enhancement of quality and the dissemination of good practice. In 1995 a working groups was set up by the Pro Vice- chancellor for Quality Assurance and Research to develop a University wide framework for review to complement external process. A University—wide Monitoring and Feedback Steering Group was established to coordinate the collection of data and to develop a strategic approach to the policy in this area. The group chaired by the Vice-Chancellor for Quality Assurance and Research.

The Institute of Education Technology of the University is responsible for the monitoring and feedback of the University's courses. It regularly undertakes student feedback surveys and all new courses are reviewed at the end of the first presatation.

The OU is a large and complex organization. In common with other universities basic units posses considerable autonomy. The twin external quality processes of subject based assessment and international level audit impact upon the work of staff in direct and indirect ways

Factors for Success

Walter Perry identifies 4 factors for the success of the Open University:

1. The fighting sprit of the staff engendered by the widespread skepticism about its success.
2. The determination, staying power and success rates of the students. The University was for many of them an emancipation.
3. The care almost pastoral in nature, that part-time tutors took over the well-being of their students both academic and otherwise;
4. The fact that all teaching was open to view by the public and by the academic world that could thus recognize the continued quality of courses.

18

Sukhothai Thammathirat Open University, Thailand

Sukhothai Thammathirat Open University (STOU) was officially established by Royal Charter on 5 September 1978 as Thailand's eleventh state university. His Majesty King Bhumibol Adulyadej (King Rama IX) graciously bestowed the university its name in honour of King Prajadhipok (King Rama VII), who once held the title "Prince Sukhothai Thammaracha" prior his accession to the throne.

On 24 October 1978, His Majesty issued royal mandates appointing the first University Council and appointing Professor Dr. Wichit Srisa-an as the first president, effective from January 1978.

From 1979 to 1984, STOU had no home campus of its own, so it had to share space with such agencies as the National Education Commission, Thai Airways, the Faculty of Economics of Chulalongkorn University, and the Ministry of University Affairs. In 1981, Mr. Monkol Kanjanapas donated to the university a 30-rai section of land located in Pakkret district of Nonthaburi province. The university then bought more land, bringing the total to approximately 135 rai. Construction at this site began in 1982, and the university began operating from the new location on 9 December 1984.

At its founding, STOU was the first university in Southeast Asia to use the distance learning system. This new system of learning expanded the role of higher education in Thailand by engaging learners who previously had no opportunity to further their education. Since its establishment, STOU has enabled the development of individuals and communities throughout Thailand and beyond.

Vision

Sukhothai Thammathirat Open University aims to be a world-class open university utilizing a distance education system to provide lifelong learning for all.

Mission

- To produce qualified graduates.
- To develop the country's human resources at all levels.
- To strengthen communities, organizations and social institutions so they can participate in a knowledge-based society.
- To research, promote and develop the body of knowledge and local indigenous wisdom available to Thai society.
- To preserve, promote and develop Thai arts and culture.

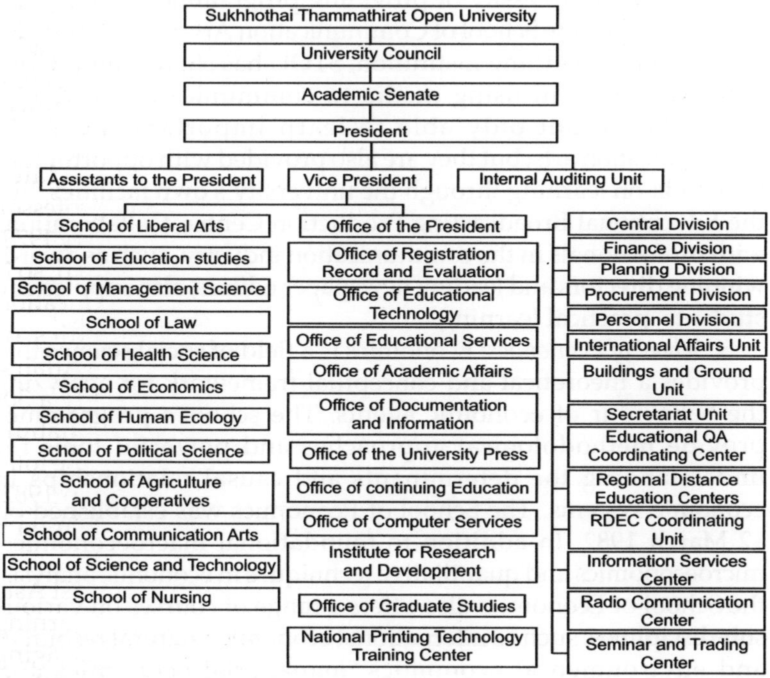

Schools

1. *School of Agriculture and Cooperatives*: The School of Agricultural Extension and Cooperatives was founded on the conviction that since agriculture has been a key livelihood for Thai people, wider economic development in Thailand is tied to development of the country's agricultural potential. The school

continues to rely on this philosophy in teaching students subjects such as agricultural production methods, agricultural technology, and the formation and management of agricultural cooperatives. In addition, the school aims to give students an understanding of Thailand's natural resources and resources for conservation through agricultural practices.

2. *School of Communication Arts*: The field of communication arts is concerned with the application of different types of media used to relay news, transfer knowledge, and provide entertainment. As effective management of these systems promotes development, increases knowledge and fosters mutual understanding, STOU recognized the necessity of providing programmes in this field, and established the School of Communication Arts in 1984. Because it is a distance learning institution, STOU has significant interest and experience in using media to communicate effectively. Students are not only able to learn important theory in communication arts, but they are also provided with opportunities for hands-on learning through the university's own facilities, like the Educational Broadcasting Production Center. Collaborations with professionals in the communication industry, such as award-winning directors and leading newspaper editors, also supplement students' practical learning.

3. *School of Economics*: Economics is a field of social science that provides a theoretical and conceptual framework for analyzing the behaviour of economic agents. The school's programmes provide methodological approaches and powerful tools for understanding the determinants and causal relationships in economic systems. The School of Economics was established on 12 March 1982. In addition to foundational macroeconomics, microeconomics and quantitative techniques in economic analysis, the School of Economics also offers a range of courses on various sub-disciplines, such as international economics, natural resources and environmental economics, managerial economics and economic development. The school aims to equip students with a sound understanding of the logic of the discipline as well as rigorous analytical skills crucial to logical decision-making processes at all levels.

4. *School of Educational Studies*: The School of Education Studies, established on 7 February 1979, offers programmes which focus on developing in-service educational personnel who can

strengthen their communities with increased academic knowledge and professional ethics. The school also aims to promote research development in the fields of teacher education and educational studies, provide academic services to educational personnel and other interested parties, and contribute to the preservation and maintenance of national arts and culture.

5. *School of Health Science*: Large numbers of public health workers in a number of fields still have a need for continuing education. To help workers oversee the more effective provision of public health services, the School of Health Science was established on 25 August 1979. With a range of programmes, from public health to environment management, students in the School of Health Science will gain crucial expertise and experience to help improve the health and living standards of the Thai people. One area the school highlights is the importance of continual personal development alongside an even as an individual works to further the development of the country.

6. *School of Human Ecology*: Established on 29 December 1981 as the School of Home Economics, the school aims to offer programmes that lead to improved living standards and quality of life for individual, family and social units. Over the years since its founding, the school has been attuned to the government's four-year National Economic and Social Development plans. As various plans have focused on areas such as rural development, coping with rapid changes and growth in business and industry, and incorporating human development into economic expansion, the school has responded by offering programmes that work towards these goals. In 2006, the name "School of Human Ecology" was adopted to better reflect the school's focus on the relationship that individuals, families and communities have with their environments.

7. *School of Law*: The School of Law was established on 19 February 1980 to support and develop personnel in legal professions in both government and private sectors. The school also has seeks to provide continuing education in the field of law for those holding degrees and diplomas in other areas, as well as for other prospective learners.

In 1993, the school set up the Center for Human Rights and Peace Education to disseminate knowledge in connection with human rights law and peace issues. In 2001, the Institute of International Economics and Business Law Studies was established to develop the legal knowledge of the school's faculty members and STOU staff provide relevant information to students and the general public.

8. *School of Liberal Arts*: The School of Liberal Arts was established on 7 February 1979 to provide general foundation courses in language, sociology humanities, Thai studies and mathematics to students in all schools of the university. The school has offered bachelor's degree programmes in Thai studies and information science since 1988 and 1993 respectively, while a graduate programme in information studies was launched in 2002. In 2005, a certificate programme in Chinese language was introduced to meet the country's demand for international communication.

Sukhothai Studies Center This special project of the School of Liberal Arts supports study and research on the old Thai kingdom of Sukhothai. The educational philosophy of Sukhothai Thammathirat Open University is to expand higher educational opportunities for people at aıl levels. This philosophy corresponds with the distinct thoughts on liberty, opportunity and equality that characterized the prosperity of Thai civilization in the Sukhothai period. Therefore, on the 700th anniversary of the invention of the Thai alphabet by King Ramkhamhaeng the Great of Sukhothai, STOU established the Sukhothai Studies Center to support study the economics, society, politics, and other aspects of the Sukhothai kingdom. The center's work also includes the promotion and maintenance of arts and culture from the Sukhothai period

9. *School of Management Science*: The School of Management Science, which was established on 7 February 1979, conducts academic research, provides academic services to the public and disseminates professional knowledge to businesspeople, government officials and administrators in various sectors. Another important aim of the school is the promotion of morality and professional ethics in the areas of administration and management. The many business and public administration programmes at the School of Management Science are popular choices for STOU students looking to participate in Thailand's development.

10. *School of Nursing*: STOU's instruction in nursing arose from a desire to expand higher educational opportunities for nurses without forcing them to leave their jobs and families. Originally, the Bachelor of Nursing programme was under the administration

of the School of Health Science until 12 July 2000, when the School of Nursing was established. A master's degree programme, which started in 2005, integrates nursing science, management science and other related topics. Students in the School of Nursing acquire new expertise while working, giving them a chance to quickly apply what they have learned. Their productivity and effectiveness are greatly boosted, and their organizations also benefit from reduced personnel development costs and fewer staffing shortages.

11. *School of Political Science*: The School of Political Science was established on 19 August 1982. One of its most unique services is to provide certificate-level courses that aim to upgrade the general public's knowledge and skills in politics and administration, which will enable them to play an important role in the development of a democratic society. These programmes are helping to engage people from different walks of life in the political life of the nation. Students are spread across the country and come from diverse backgrounds, so instruction highlights the social implications of politics and its role in Thai society and government.

12. *School of Science and Technology*: STOU officially established the School of Science and Technology on 12 July 2000 after extensive preparations. The school provides opportunities for working professionals to develop their capabilities in the fields of printing technology and information technology. As students and graduates apply their knowledge and abilities in their respective careers, Thai society gains a greater understanding and appreciation of technology. STOU's National Printing Technology Training Center is an important resource for STOU students in the Printing Technology programme, as they undertake training in printing and bookbinding procedures at the center.

Examination Centers

To make assessment affordable and convenient for students, STOU has set up at least one examination center in each province, though many provinces have more than one site. Inmates of corrective institutions who have been granted permission to register as students may take their examinations in their respective institutions. STOU students residing abroad are able to take examinations at the local Royal Thai Embassy or Consulate. Local study center personnel and university staff members coordinate in supervising the examinations.

Student Enrolment

Schools	*Students*
Agricultural Extension and Cooperatives	9,672
Communication Arts	3,814
Economics	1,662
Educational Studies	5,989
Health Science	12,099
Human Ecology	5,179
Law	25,430
Liberal Arts	11,494
Management Science	55,798
Nursing	473
Political Science	19,937
Science and Technology	5,451
Total	**156,998**

Technology Use

Asynchronous Communication	*Synchronous Communication*
Blogs	Chatrooms
E-mail	Instant messaging (e.g. ICQ, MSN)
Microblogging (e.g. Twitter)	Online forums (eg Eluminate)
Online Forums/Threaded discussions	Shared Whiteboards
Personal Portals (e.g. iGoogle)	Teleconferencing
Podcasts	Telephone
RSS feeds	Video Conferencing
Shared Calendars/Meeting Scheduling (e.g. Doodle)	Virtual workspaces
SMS/MMS	Voice-over IP (e.g. Skype)
Social Networking Utilities (e.g. Facebook, MySpace)	
Vidcasts	
Voicemail	
Webinars	
Website	
Wikis	

Examination Schedule

Since STOU does not want students to give up their work or leave aside their official duties, examinations are held on weekends and are arranged so that they can be completed in two days. Final examinations are held at the end of each semester, and a subsequent of make-up examinations for students who failed or missed the final examinations.

Criteria for Evaluation

Master's Degree

For master's degree programmes the university evaluates students from the results of the following:

- Assigned work
- Semester examinations
- Thesis examinations for Plan A or comprehensive and independent study examinations for Plan
- Graduate Professional Experience workshop

Bachelor's Degree

Course blocks are divided into two types: theory courses and practical courses. Written examination results make up at least 80 per cent of the grade for theory courses. For practical courses, grading is based on the makeup and requirements of each individual course.

Why Study at STOU?

- STOU programmes lead to degrees and qualifications that improve students' lives. Every degree programme taught at STOU has been approved by the Ministry of University Affairs. Furthermore, the Office of the Civil Service Commission has affirmed that all degrees from STOU hold the same honours, rights and privileges as those from conventional universities.
- Students can study without taking time out from working. STOU students are able to continue pursuing their careers while studying in STOU degree programmes.
- Students can study in other educational institutions at the same time. STOU students can study in other educational institutions at the same time that they are enrolled in STOU because they don't have to conform to a classroom schedule. Instead, they are able to study on their own, according to the demands of their lives. Being able to gain academic or professional experience outside of the STOU programme greatly increases the value of a degree from STOU, opening up a broader range of opportunities upon completion.
- An STOU education is affordable. Expenses for STOU students are significantly lower than in conventional universities, because students do not have extra expenses such as travel costs, room and board, uniforms and course materials.

- Studying at STOU is convenient. STOU students can study from home, or anywhere else for that matter. They can learn through a combination of resources, including home-based materials and media, libraries, study centers and face-to-face tutorial sessions. Final examinations and makeup exams are conveniently administered in every province, and tasks such as registration can be completed by mail, telephone, internet or even through bank branches.
- An STOU education provides freedom. STOU students are free to set a study schedule and style that fits with their readiness, availability and any other factors that have an impact on their lives.
- Course materials are relevant and useful. STOU's detailed and complete course materials are developed by qualified faculty and specialists to be accessible and easy to understand on their own, without the need for additional instruction or explanation.
- STOU programmes are accessible to the elderly and the disabled. Applicants age 60 and up are eligible for a discount in the cost of their studies at STOU. STOU works with disabled students (over 250 in 2010) by providing special services and developing appropriate alternative study materials such as audio textbooks.

Distance Learning System

Studies at STOU are not confined to traditional classrooms. The STOU distance learning system makes quality higher education accessible to all, providing students with the freedom to study and interact according to their individual circumstances and locations. Courses are developed by course teams and then delivered to students through distance media. STOU has one main campus for administrators and instructors as well as an extensive network of study and service centers throughout the country.

Study Methods and Instructional Media

The accessibility of STOU's study programmes is maximized through the broad variety of educational media the university uses. The array of educational media makes STOU's distance education programmes accessible to people in widely varying socio-economic backgrounds and geographic locations. The variety of media and study methods also encourages interaction between students and university personnel. Originally, the main teaching materials were textbooks and workbooks mailed to students. Now, the university follows the STOU Plan 2000 in providing distance education courses. According to this plan, course blocks can be presented in two ways: print-based and computer-based (e-learning). As technological capabilities increase throughout the country, STOU continually explores opportunities to implement new media.

Print-based: For print-based courses, textbooks and workbooks are mailed to students along with other course documents. Supplementary audiovisual materials may be included as well. For maximum accessibility, most STOU programmes are print-based, but they still make use of the full array of supplementary media listed below.

Computer-based: Though STOU has been involved with implementing e-learning (the use of computers in education) since 1985, it wasn't until the STOU Plan 2000 was adopted that the university outlined a clear plan for delivering the main content of study programmes via e-learning.

2005 marked the first large-scale online learning project at STOU. ATutor was chosen as the Learning Management System (LMS). In 2009, D4L was introduced as another LMS option.

When the main media is computer-based currently use the D4L+P platform. They contain the same number of units as print-based courses, but the online environment allows more collaboration and student-teacher interaction. The units (called modules) contain both individual and group tasks.

Radio and TV broadcasts

Radio and TV broadcasts are a unique and valuable part of STOU courses. Five radio and five television programmes are provided for each course block. The programmes are usually produced in STOU's Educational Broadcasting Production Center.

Summary of STOU Instructional Media

- Main Media

Print-based Approach

- Textbooks
- Workbooks (undergraduate courses)
- Study guides (graduate courses)

Computer-based Approach

- Online LMS
- Course materials on CD ROM mirror those available online
- Supplementary Media
- Radio programmes
- Public television programmes
- STOU Channel—the university's own C-band satellite TV station
- Satellite radio
- Audio tapes/CDs—recordings of radio programmes
- Video CDs/DVDs—recordings of TV programmes
- Media on demand—audiovisual resources available through the STOU website
- Online e-learning resources
- Multimedia CDs—offline e-learning resources, mirroring those online
- Tutorial sessions—face-to-face interaction; also via webcast, satellite video link
- E-tutorials—recordings of tutorials accessible through the university website
- M-learning—resources tailored for study via mobile devices; under ongoing development

Material Production and Dissemination

All key hard-copy study materials (mostly textbooks and workbooks) are mailed to students each semester. The textbooks go through at least two revisions before being printed by the university press. Finally, the books and other materials are sent to students by the Office of Educational Services.

Sukhothai Thammathirat Open University or STOU students study by themselves with utmost independence. Like other conventional public universities, STOU is under the control of the Ministry of University Affairs, and has the right to award its own degrees. To provide academic support for independent study, the University has established various types of academic services. One of such services is the provision of library and information services.

Library and Information Services

ODI organised three levels of library and information services for STOU students, namely central, regional and provincial services.

Each level of services has established with the following responsibilities.

1. *Central Services*: The Central services are provided through the Office of Documentation and Information in the Documentation Building and the Academic Building I at Nonthaburi. Its main purpose is to make resources available to STOU faculty staff members and course teams, STOU staff members, researchers and the general public who wish to use library materials and access to information. However, STOU students may access library and information services at ODI while attending activities and seminars on the university campus. Graduate students may be approached for assistance in finding information and making photocopying of library materials with free of charge through mail, fax and e-mail.

A variety of services available from the University's library. Some examples of basic library services are as follows:

1. Reference and information service
2. Loan service
3. Inter-library loan service
4. Information access and retrieval
5. Photocopying Service
6. Orientation and library visits

At the central services, computers and information technology have been used for a wide range of library functions. Currently, six modules of the VTLS library automation systems, namely acquisition, cataloguing, circulation, OPAC, serial control and journal indexing are in use. In addition, the library automation system of the ODI is able to link together the various STOU computer systems, and the national and international institutions of higher learning. This will enable ODI to expand its services and to provide more effective and efficient library services to the students through long-distance requests.

2. *Regional Services*: There are two types of library services at regional level. They are library services of the Academic and Development Services Centers and Graduate Educational Resource Centers.

Library Services of the Academic and Development Services Centers

According to the University's plan 10 Academic and Development

Services Centers will be established throughout the different region—the northern, central, northeastern, eastern and southern. Currently, nine Centers are in operation. Each library of the Center serves as a repository and service center with up-to-date library materials. In the near future, each Center will install a computer network system. This computer system will facilitate communication links and the exchange of information, both within and outside the University. A sub-system of library automation system is also placed in a plan.

The following library services are the basic services provided for STOU students and the general public:

1. Reference and information service
2. Loan service
3. Inter-library loan service
4. Information access and retrieval
5. Photocopying Service

Graduate Educational Resource Centers

With the purpose to establish library services centers for graduate students of STOU, six Graduate Educational Resource Centers were set up with the cooperation of various government agencies in 1993.

In each Graduate Educational Resource Center, self-instructional materials, reference books and textbooks for graduate students are available. It is the responsible of the ODI to supply such materials as well as to develop the library services system and producing finding aids and tools.

The following library services are provided to STOU graduate students:

1. Reference and information service
2. Loan service
3. Photocopying service

Provincial Services

Provincial Services are offered in the *STOU Corners* located in 75 provincial public libraries through the cooperation of the Department of Non-formal Education. The University has also received cooperation from the Bangkok Metropolitan in establishing *STOU Corners* in four public libraries in Bangkok, namely the

Lumpini Park, the Soi Phra Nang, the Phasicharoen and the Bang Khen public libraries. In addition, Mahawachirawut School in Songkhla province has also given its cooperation by establishing a STOU Corner in Tinnasulanon Library. Similar services also provided in the Bang Khwang Central Prison, Nonthaburi.

Each STOU Corner acts as a repository and services center of different types of selected materials and media prepared by the ODI in order to provide a service which will be of benefits to the University undergraduate students and the general public in local area.

The following library services are provided:

1. Reference and information service
2. Loan service

The Use of Information Technology for Library and Information Services

The following are the examples of the electronic library services provided to the staff members at the central service.

1. *On-line public Access Catalogue*: Since 1991 the on-line public catalogue has been made for both Thai and English materials available at the ODI. The academic staff could access the catalogue on campus and through the ODI Web page (www.odi.stou.ac.th).

2. *CD-ROM Databases*: The ODI has subscribed to various databases of different areas in the form of CD-ROM. A CD-ROM network was set up in 1996. Currently the databases available to the staff and students include ERIC, ADO, SIC and Laser Quest.

3. *Internet*: Through the STOU computer system, the users are able to access information from the Internet at the ODI.

4. *Specific Databases*: The university has largely succeeded in providing lifelong education to the people of different social strata. It has democratised education by providing educational opportunities to the maximum number of people.

All those who are unable to get into conventional universities get into the advantage of higher education at reduced costs. Its teaching methods are scientific and highly technology mediated. The University has become a leader to many higher educational institutions in Thailand. Rapid human recourses development is taking place by the skills provided by various courses of the University.

19

University of South Africa

Founded in 1873 as the University of Cape of Good Hope, the University of South Africa (or Unisa as it is commonly known) spent most of its early history as an examining agency for Oxford and Cambridge universities and as incubator from which most other universities in South Africa are descended. In 1946, it was given a new role as a distance education university and today it offers certificate, diploma and degree courses up to doctoral level....

In January 2004, Unisa merged with Technikon Southern Africa (formally known as Technikon SA) and incorporated the distance education component of Vista University. The combined institution retained the name University of South Africa, unlike other merged institutions, which underwent name changes.

Unisa's Muckleneuk Campus is located in Pretoria and is a major landmark of the capital city. It was in 1972 that Unisa is moved into its new home on Muckleneuk Ridge having vacated the old quarters in central Pertoria. The complex of buildings was designed by Bryan Sandrock Architects in the 1960s and expresses an international style characterized by cantilevered structures. The most striking feature is the long projection from the brow of the hill, supported by against steel girder resting on a massive column

Students and Staff

According to the Department of Institutional Statistics and Analysis (DISA) at the university, Unisa had 328,179 students enrolled in 2011 from South African, and others international states. The largest portion of these students are South African, being 91.5 per cent (300,211) of the sum of the students enrollments. The majority of these students enrolled at the College of Economic and

Management Sciences (CEMS), being 42.5 per cent (139,358) of the sum of the student enrollment.

Unisa had 5,575 staff member in 2011. The majority of the staff employed are non-professional administrative staff, being 56.8 per cent (3,168). The number of institutional/research professionals are 33.2 per cent (1,846) of the sum of the staff employed.

Academic Community

As an open Distance Learning (ODL) institution, and one of the world's mega universities, Unisa presents academic offerings associated with both technological and traditional universities. These include, but are not limited to, a combination of career-oriented courses usually associated with a university of technology, and formative academic programmes typically to a traditional university.

- College of Accounting Sciences
- College of Agricultural and Environmental Science
- College of Education
- College of Economic and Management Science
- College of Graduate Studies
- College of Human Sciences
- College of Law
- College of Science, Engineering and Technology
- Graduate School of Business Leadership (SBL)

In addition to the eight colleges and SBL, Unisa has numerous Bureaus, Centers, Institutes, Museums and Units supporting academic development and research.

Ranking

In 2013 University of South Africa was ranked as a 6th best university in Africa and 862nd in the world according to the Webometrics.

Culture

Unisa has been promoting and promulgating culture in all its manifestations since its inception in 1873. Apart from the academic courses offered by Unisa's college of Humanities, practical languages, art and music skills have been actively pursued through the settings of curricula and the implementation of special courses and examinations.

- Africa Center for Arts Culture and Heritage studies
- Museum of Anthropology and Archaeology
- Department of Music
- Unisa Space Art Gallery
- Unisa Music Foundation

2015 Strategic Plan of the University

Open Distance Learning Policy

- The 2015 strategic plan of University of South Africa (UNISA) dedicated itself to becoming the African University in service humanity.
- UNISA commits itself to advancing social justice with an emphasis on redress, equity and empowerment of the previously disadvantaged groups in South Africa such as blacks, women, people with disabilities, the rural and urban poor and adults generally who have missed out on opportunities to access higher education.
- UNISA is South Africa's only comprehensive dedicated distance education university. The conceptualization of distance education and open learning is central to achieving its vision.

Principles

UNISA is a comprehensive open distance learning institution that will:

- Increase the participation of student and access to post-registration student support services.
- Diversify the body of students for the purpose of providing opportunities for social advancement for historically and socially disadvantaged social groups such as students in rural areas, small town to those who do not have convenient access to higher education institutions.
- Provide quality education in an affordable and cost-effective way.
- Encourage and support temporarily inactive students, monitor retention and throughput and implement the necessary interventions for improvement.
- Develop its capacity in distance education delivery through reflective practice including staff development processes.
- Engage in research and development of open distance practices and contribute extensively to national debate in this area.

- Start the teaching process with the development of curriculum long before the student register. This will enable better pre-registration decision-making for students as well as the development of more coherent programmes by academics.
- Offer the full range of qualification listed on the new HEQF in its PQM and provide articulation pathways to allow maximum portability and progression between qualifications as befits a comprehensive university.

Effective Counseling and Guidance

- A decentralized, technology supported, guidance and counseling service will be provide to assist students in making appropriate career decisions and in choosing study programmes that will help them realize their career goals.
- Students will be assisted during their studies and on their exit from the University to prepare for entry into the world of work.
- Decentralized academic development service will be provided to assist students in acquiring a range of academic literacy.

Responsible Open Admission Procedures

- UNISA will adhere to responsible open admission policy.
- This process provide for the assessment of student' levels of academic preparedness and aims to design appropriate support systems for students who need help in addressing academic skills gaps. Social preconditions for successful study will also receive attention. These will be provided through actions such as foundation courses, extended programmes, academic literacy skills facilitation, as well as orientation to studying at a distance.
- The support system for students will balance issues of openness with statutory accreditation requirements and governmental enrolment targets.

Teaching and Learning Methods

The ODL teaching and learning methods for a particular programme or courses:

- Will be determined by the nature of the programme, the profile of the students, student's access to resources and the HEQF level of the programme.
- Will include independent study of learning materials, completion of various activities, formative assessment tasks,

tutorials, practical work and opportunities to interact with others as well as research activities.

Learning Material

- Will be systematically designed as outlined in the Tuition Policy and Framework for a Team Approach to Curriculum and Learning Development.
- Will be accessible to target students.
- Will require the active engagement of the student.
- Will build the students' experience and knowledge enabling the student to construct new knowledge.

UNISA will make effective use of educational and social technologies in learning programmes in appropriate and innovative ways that improve the quality of teaching and learning

Delivery Channels

- Advanced teaching and learning models, well designed courseware, effective/efficient administration and timeous students support using a wide range of delivery channels are core to the success of our students. Unisa will use the best possible mix of media to support these core functions which include:

Print Media

- Print media remains the practical choice since it is inexpensive, reliable and accepted as a medium for studying purpose.
- Courseware should be well designed to facilitate access to information.
- Courseware material should prepare the student for learning, develop the necessary skills, attitude and knowledge that the student need, guide the student through the learning process and include sufficient and appropriate learning activities to enhance knowledge.
- Unisa will invest in good quality course design and study material and will provide in-text student support services.

Technologies with Limited Interaction

- Others resources such as digital media (audio and video cassettes, CDs, DVDs) satellite broadcasting, online distribution of content and information via my Unisa and corporate websites, audio and video podcasting and streaming, and possibly radio and television will also be used to facilitate the process of teaching and learning.

- Some of the technologies that are asynchronous such as wikis, blogs, social nerworking facilities and e-portfolios can be used effectively to support teaching and learning

Multimedia with Interactive Possibilities

- Diverse and current technologies that will serve Unisa's educational mission and be sustainable will be included in the delivery of courseware. Technologies such as telephony, multimedia CDs and DVDs, video and audio conferencing, SMSs and MMSs via cell phones, email and discussing forms/ chat facilities via my Unisa offer new possibilities for supporting innovative learning in distance education and must be integrated from the design phase of courseware. These various options are used to facilitate interaction in support of the courseware. Highly interactive multi-party engagement can use:
  (a)Well equipped facilities for face- to-face contact sessions, and
  (b) Many of the above technologies in combination with rich media and multi-direction, multi-user, collaborative toolsets in a distributed web-based environment
- Unisa uses advanced synchronous technologies which range from web based document and application sharing, online whiteboards combined with audio/video and texting facilities, interactive assessment, to simulations and virtual reality.
- The multimedia approach with interactivity between student and lecturer(s), students and tutors, students and students, and students and institution is much more effective than a single medium. Criteria for the selection of media include:
  - ➢ Access and availability
  - ➢ Pedagogical appropriateness
  - ➢ Integration of the media into a coherent experience.

Student Support

- Takes into consideration the diverse needs of students as well as the level of study
- Is a critical factor for teaching, learning and research in open distance learning.

- Encompasses tuition, peer, in-text and administrative support and the orientation to work—integrated learning. Tuition support include detailed, formative and timely feedback on students' assignments via the decentralizes distribution of assignments as well as opportunities to engage in argument and debate with their peers and tutors through a variety of accessible and appropriate media, such as face-to-face, telematic and online. The regions will play crucial role in providing facilities for tuition and peer support as well as access to library materials
- Includes mechanisms designed to bride the gap between student's learning experience from high school and the demands of higher education, or between undergraduate and postgraduate studies,
- Enhances communication between the student and the lecturer(s), student and peers, student and courseware, student and administrative support and student and institution.

Assessment

Assessment is central to student learning and fundamentally influences the way students respond to courses and behave as students.

The assessment strategy:

- Will ensure that students develop effective cognitive, reflective, self-management and practical skills.
- Will include formative assessment which is designed to support the teaching and learning processes or support research skills.
- Will include formative and summative assessment aspects that will be used for making a judgment about the achievement of the learning outcomes.
- Will assist students and tutors to monitor their learning in relation to formative assessment task and feedback.

Regional Infrastructure and Decentralized Services

- The regional infrastructure will provide the platform for the provision of a range of student support and administrative structures.
- The decentralized regional structure bridges the gap between the university and its students.
- Regional network will provide an expanding range of services to students such as access to facilities for both independent and

group-based study and discussion, material collection, library facilities, computer facilities, councellors, tutors and literacy development.

- Regional center will also arrange for facilities for limited contact classes and manage decentralized tutoring.
- Unisa will constantly review and develop these regional and decentralized services, including access to and support in the use of emerging technologies.
- Regional offices will assist with the placements of students for work-integrated learning

Research

- Unisa is committed to scholarly teaching in ODL as well as the scholarship of teaching and learning
- Reflective research is an extremely important component of ODL research.
- Research in ODL can assist in:
    - ➢ Describing and analyzing current trends.
    - ➢ Revealing challenges and obstacles to ODL effectiveness in delivery.
    - ➢ Investigating potential contributions of ODL to socio-economic development.
    - ➢ Evaluating ODL programmes and building models that work in the South African ODL context.
    - ➢ Formulating ODL theoretical explanations for ODL phenomena.
    - ➢ Identifying strategies to improve student throughout.
    - ➢ Evaluating impact of ODL practices
- Through research Unisa will constantly reflect on teaching and support services in order to improve practice.

Academic Collaborations

- Unisa collaborates with distance education institutions in South Africa, Africa and internationally to make opportunities available for employees and students
- Collaboration is an important strategy for renewal and development in ODL
- Academic collaborations are a common strategy for capacity building.

20

Universitas Terbuka, Indonesia

Universitas Terbuka (UT, literally Open University) is Indonesia's 45th state university and employs open and distance learning (ODL) system to widen access to higher education to all Indonesian citizens, including those who live in remote islands throughout the country as well as in various parts of the world. It has a total student body of more than 460,000.

Mission

UT's focus is on educating people who for various reasons including lack of funding, rural isolation and full-time employment, do not have opportunity to attend conventional face-to-face higher education institutions.

The University's mission is:

1. to expand the opportunity for quality higher education through the distance education system;
2. to produce competent academicians and professionals who are able to compete globally;
3. to increase participation in continuing education in order to create a knowledge-based society;
4. to increase the quality and quantity of research and development in the distance education system, especially in distance higher education;
5. to innovatively and continuously disseminate and share information on distance education especially on distance higher education;
6. to strengthen national unity and integrity through the broad and equal provision of higher education;

7. to increase cross-cultural understanding and networking through local, national and global partnerships;
8. to produce academic products in distance higher education as well as in other fields of knowledge.

Flexible Learning

UT offers a learning flexibility system:

- no time limitation to complete the study, i.e. no dropout system;
- no time limitation on the year of graduation from senior high school, thus no age limit;
- all year-round registration period;
- flexible phase, place and time to study in accordance with student's own convenience;
- use of multimedia learning materials, including printed learning materials accompanied by audio and video cassettes/CD, CD-ROM, radio and TV broadcast, as well as Computer-Assisted Instructions (CAI) and Internet-based learning materials.

Learning Materials

Learning activities can be conducted at anywhere and any time.

Printed material (known as module) serves as the main learning medium, supplemented by non-printed materials such as recorded learning materials (audio video cassettes, CD, radio and TV), as well as computer based learning materials (CAI and Internet based). UT assures the high quality of its learning materials.

Learning Support Service

The learning support services consist of academic and administrative services.

Academic Services: The academic services are provided through tutorials. There are two kinds of tutorials: face-to-face and at a distance via radio, television, and internet. Furthermore, practical works are also provided for courses that need practicum. Both tutorials and practical works are facilitated by qualified tutors, instructors, and or supervisors, who come from various well-known public and private universities as well as from UT itself. For certain courses, resource persons are sometimes invited from business, industry and other relevant sectors.

Administrative Services Administrative services are emphasized in providing assistance to students in registration, obtaining learning materials, applying for credit transfer, and addressing other matters that can influence students' study process.

Student Assessment

The assessment of student learning is based on: tutorial assignments, practical works, practicum assignments, and final examination. These components reflect students' overall learning achievement and contribute to the semester final grades of the students.

UT administers final examinations at the end of every semester or twice a year. Final examinations are conducted as supervised pencil-paper tests simultaneously throughout the country. Students who take the Bachelor (Sarjana/S1) Programmes are required to take the Program's Final Assignment at the end of the programme as part of the requirements. Students who take the Master Programmes (S2) are required to write Master Program's Final Assignment (a thesis) and pass the final oral examination. For certain courses and cases UT also offers the opportunity for students to take the examination on-line.

Final grades are announced via various methods including through UT website, and UPBJJ-UT.

Credit Transfer

UT students may apply for credit transfer for courses previously taken from other accredited universities.

Operational Networking

UT has 37 regional offices, known as UPBJJ-UT, in 32 provinces. To support their operations, each UPBJJ-UT establishes close collaboration with various institutions, particularly with:

- The local public and private universities for getting tutors, practicum instructors, and examination supervisors;
- Local governments for conducting tutorials and examination, as well as for getting scholarships for students; and
- Local radio and TV stations for relaying the tutorials and information about academic activities. The regular tutorials broadcast by the national radio stations (RRI).

At the national level, UT also has long standing collaborations with:

- Q-Channel and TV-Edukasi for broadcasting UT's TV programmes;

- RRI for broadcasting radio tutorials;
- BRI and BTN for receiving tuition fees and learning materials purchase from students; and
- PT Pos Indonesia for delivering the learning materials, examination documents and other supporting materials.

Academic Programme

UT has four Faculties and one Graduate Programme that offer more than 30 Study Programmes, including Master Programmes (S2), Bachelor Programmes (Sarjana/S1), Diploma Programmes (D1, D2, D3, and D4), and Certificate Programmes.

Faculty of Teacher Training and Educational Sciences

Bachelor (S1) Programmes

Indonesian and Literature Education; English Education; Mathematics Education; Physics Education; Chemistry Education; Biology Education; Economics Education; Pancasila and Civics Education; Primary School Teacher Education; Early Childhood Education Teacher

Certificate Programmes

Indonesian for Foreigners; Public Administration of District Area

Faculty of Social and Political Sciences

Bachelor (S1) Programmes

Public Administration; Business Administration; Government Studies; Communication Science; Sociology; Law; English Translation

Diploma 4 (D4) Program

Archive

Diploma 3 (D3) Program

Taxation

Diploma 2 (D2) Program

Library Science

Faculty of Economics

Bachelor (S1) Program

Economics Development; Management; Accounting

Faculty of Mathematics and Natural Sciences

Bachelor (S1) Program

Mathematics; Statistics; Biology; Agribusiness, Majoring in Agricultural Extension and Communication/Animal Husbandry/ Fishery; Food Technology and Science

Diploma 1 (D1) Program

Environmental Management

Graduate Programmes

Master (S2) Programmes

Administration Science, majoring in Public Administration; Management; Marine Science, majoring in Fishery Management; Mathematics Education

Human Resource Development Services

UT offers the following programmes: Upgrading qualifications of human resource in:

Public Administration; Business Administration; Government Studies; Communication Studies; Taxation Studies; Language Services; Management, Accounting Studies; Economics and Development Studies; Applied Statistics, Mathematics, and Science; Food Technology; Agricultural Extension Programmes

Education and Training for Managers and Instructors

Training needs analysis; Making plans for training center; Developing learning materials, either printed or electronic; Providing in-house training, either face-to-face or at a distance; Training programme Evaluation

Multimedia Production Facilities

UT has a Multimedia Production Center with facilities and human resources. The staffs are professionally trained in audio visual development and production in Indonesia and overseas.[citation needed] Several government and private institutions have utilized this, company profiles, promotions, and learning materials in the form of video, audio-tape, audio-graphics, slides, and VCD.

Research and Development

The Center for Research and Community Services of UT (LPPM-UT) has four centers:

- Center of Institutional Research and System Development
- Center of Science
- Center of Community Services
- Inter-University Center for Improving and Developing Instructional Activities (IUC-IDIA)

Research: The LPPM-UT specializes research and development in the following areas:

- Open and Distance Education
- Evaluation of Educational
- Educational Management
- Policy and Institutional Studies
- Social Development
- Regional Economic Development
- Environmental Impact Analysis
- Regional Development
- Agriculture, Fishery, and Husbandry
- Sciences
- Instructional Media
- Consultancy and Research Training
- Monitoring and Evaluation

Development of Management Information System LPPM-UT provides:

- Management Information System Design.
- Application of Computerized Management Information
- Systems Application
- website Design and Development
- Information Systems Development
- Information Systems Evaluation
- Media Prototype Development

Community Services Community services include:

- Training for continuing education programmes.
- Development of people's empowerment programmes to improve the quality of life.

- Development of networks and partnerships to support the continuing education and social services programmes.
- Professional consultancy services in people's empowerment, human resource, education, and development of both organization and society.

Development and Improvement of Instructions

The Inter-University Center for Improving and Developing of Instructional Activities (IUC-IDIA) has a mission to improve the quality of instruction at higher levels of education at open and distance higher education and conventional universities. The IUC-IDIA professional staff have experience in conducting needs analysis, developing programmes, curriculum development, assessment of learning, evaluating instructional programmes, developing the prototype of learning materials, developing multi-media course materials, developing computer-based tutorials, and professional training for educators, trainers, and instructor.

The IUC-IDIA services include:

- Programmes for Improving the Basic Skills of Instructional Techniques (PEKERTI)
- Applied Approach (AA)
- Development of Distance Learning Systems
- Curriculum Development
- Learning Materials Development
- Tutor's Training
- Instructional Media Development
- Development of Computer-Assisted Tutorial
- Achievement Evaluation
- Classroom Action Research

The IUC-IDIA also provides consulting services for institution capacity building in education and training, particularly in the area of instructional activities and academic programmes.

The IUC-IDIA has strategic alliances with other units within UT itself, with over 51 state-owned universities, and with education and training centers in 25 Departments, Colleges belonged to certain governmental departments, as well as education and training centers for specific fields (e.g. Banking, department stores, supermarkets, etc.)

Atwi Superman, Assistant Rector of the University suggested 10 suggestions for the effective development of the University:

1. Addition of more academic programmes to meet the demand of the governments development efforts.
2. Intensive Development of learning materials and tests.
3. Enrolment and registration of students to be alone at more places.
4. Speedy distribution of learning materials to reach students' home.
5. Number of learning materials distributed to students as per their capability to learn credits.
6. Increasing the quality of tutors and recruiting local state university teachers and professionals as tutors.
7. Encouraging students to form study groups.
8. Development of own lab systems at study centres and local institutions for science practicals.
9. Increasing the frequency of examinations for students' convenience
10. Increase in Computer systems at the University headquarters and local centres.

21

National Open University of Taiwan

The establishment of the National Open University (NOU) is the major landmark in the development of distance education in Taiwan. Following a revision of the University Law in July 1982 and a Ministry of Education experimental project involving the provision of several university level distance courses between 1983 and 1986, the NOU was established in 1986, with first year courses starting in November 1986.

Organization

NOU comprises working units, some with sub-units. The major units comprise teaching, administrative and support units and regional learning centres. Seven teaching units include six academic departments and one academic group. The six academic departments are:

1. Department of Liberal Arts
2. Department of Social Sciences
3. Department Arts and Commerce
4. Department of Public Administration
5. Department of Living Sciences
6. Department of Management and Information

The administrative units are similar to those in other universities (personnel office, budgeting and accounting office, and departments of academic affairs, student affairs and general affairs). The supporting units—the publishing centre, library, computer centre and departments of educational media and of research and development and also thirteen regional learning centres. These units have undergone changes owing to the need for reorganization and expansion.

NOU has both full-time and contract staff. Most full-time staff members are required to take administrative responsibilities either at the headquarters or in regional learning centres.

Students

NOU has three types of students: regular, non-diploma and auditing. A regular student must pass an entrance examination and hold a high school graduate diploma or equivalent and may apply to graduate. Students not fulfilling these requirements or simply writing to study with NOU may become non-diploma students. These students receive certificates of course credit for individual courses, but are not usually eligible for graduation. Auditing students, who study NOU courses without informing the University, do not receive certificates.

Courses, Teaching Methods and Media

NOU operates a semester system. Each course lasts one semester.

Broadcasting, print and face-to-face tutoring are the three main methods used for teaching, with broadcasting component used as a measure of the course load. One course credit is equal to eighteen broadcast episodes, each episode being 30 minutes. The majority of courses comprise three course credits, although courses with two or four course credits are also offered.

Television is the main broadcasting medium. Radio is used in some courses. Television episodes are broadcast through UHF. Television programmes are directly used to make video cassettes. Sound tracks of radio programmes are used to make audio cassettes for supplementary material for students.

Each course has a printed textbook, developed and edited in-house. Additionally, a student newsletter is published which contain broadcasting schedules, university announcements, assignment questions and a range of supplementary readings. NOU also collaborates with two newspapers which publish to NOU columns.

Face-to-face teaching, once per month and four times per semester, is an important element of all courses. Laboratory hours in regional learning centres are included in computing course.

Student assessment is through assignments and examinations. Students submit several assignments and sit mid-term and final examination to earn course credits.

NOU is in the process of transformation, particularly in management, recruitment of students and u se of media. These changes are triggered by range of external forces, of which the main one is the threat posed by other higher education institutions. Rapid developments in conventional higher education institutions in relation to distance education provision also challenge the survival of NOU.

Three main developments are computer-based distance teaching, expansion of the provision of extension education and introduction of a scheme of pre-study.

Many changes are taking place in NOU, mainly in the three areas: 1) the promotion of university autonomy, 2) multiplicity in the use of media, and 3) greater openness.

The establishment of NOU was a major milestone, followed by the two municipal open universities and served conventional higher education institutions. The most recent developments in distance education in the country are influenced by the developments in media and by economic, political and educational developments. Distance education is currently moving towards openness, flexibility and decentralization. For NOU, these developments mean more competition. NOU is in position to grow effectively and efficiently.

Key Areas of Open Universities

22
Technology

The most evident advantages of ICTs are the following (Ross H Paul):

- increased productivity;
- increased efficiency;
- innovation and product leadership;
- better quality of service;
- better decision making;
- better management and coordination;
- better staff development and training.

ICTs have been used mainly for three educational purposes (Hilary Perraton):

- to widen access to education;
- to raise its quality;
- to reform it.

Development of New Technologies in Teaching since 1980

Bates has listed 27 technological development since the 1980s:

- Audio cassettes
- Video cassettes
- Computer based learning
- Cable TV
- View data
- Teletext
- Video conferencing
- Electronic mail
- Computer conference
- Internet
- Virtual reality
- World wide web
- Digital video discs
- Fiber optics
- Learning objects
- Portals
- Simulations
- Satellite T V
- Compact discs
- LCD projectors
- Search engines
- Mobile phone

- Audio conferencing
- Audio graphics systems
- Laser video discs
- Wireless network
- e-portfolios
- Expert systems

Types of Technologies

Lewis distinguished three main technologies: (1) audio technologies, (2) video technologies, and (3) computer based technologies. A further distinction is the mode of utilisation which can be either one way (non-interactive mode) or two way (interactive mode).

Mason classified technologies used in distance education into four:

- Text-based systems, including electronic mail, computer conferencing, real-time chat system, fax and many uses of the web.
- Audio-based systems such as audio conferencing and audio graphics and audio on the web.
- Video-based systems such as video conferencing one way and two way, video on the internet with products like CU See ME, web-casting and other visual media such as video clips with web.
- The web, which integrates text, audio and video, both as pre-prepared clips as live interactive systems, both real time and stored to be accessed later and furthermore which provides text-based interactive as well as access to educational resources of unprecedented magnitude.

According to Tylor distance education operations have evolved through four generations with reference to the application of communication technologies: first, the Correspondence Model based on print technology; second, the Multi-Media based on print, audio and video technologies; third, the Telelearning Model based on application of telecommunication technologies to provide opportunities for synchronous communication; and fourth, the Flexible Learning Model based on online delivery via internet. Now emerging is the fifth generation based on further exploitation of new technologies.

Different Forms of Audio, Video and Computer Technologies

Audio Technologies

- Radio

- Audio cassettes
- Audio graphics
- Audio conferencing
- Telephone

Video Technologies

- Television
- Video cassette
- Video disc
- Compact disc
- Video text
- Teleconferencing

Computer Technologies

- Teaching via computer
- Computer conference
- Web based computer conference
- Internet
- World wide web

Audio technologies are cheap, easy to use, accessible and generally educationally effective. Hence Schramm, called audio-based technologies 'little media'. Compared with print, the human voice can have an informal quality that is not easily transmitted in print. The human voice can be modulated. It contains variations in pitch, tone, pace, volume and emphasis, which are invaluable to the learning process.

Computer is a versatile device of modern communication and information technology. It can be used for a variety of purposes and situations. Although computer gets its name originally from the power to process long and complex numerical calculations, it now serves a wide range of functions. As computer processing power increases, it becomes possible to perform many tasks.

Selection of Technologies

Jack Koumi provided a scheme of three stage media selection:

- Listing comparative merits and distinctive teaching functions.
- Devising a procedure for media deployment based on the listing.
- Fully exploiting the potential of each medium.

He further stressed that multiple media presentations can accommodate individual difference in learning.

Strengths and Weakness of Different Technologies

Technology	*Strengths*	*Weakness*
Print	Can be inexpensive Reliable Carries dense information Learner-controlled	May seen passive May need longer Production time and Significant cost
Audio/Video recordings	Dynamic Give vicarious experience Learner controlled	High development Time/costs
Radio/television	Dynamic Immediacy Mass distribution	Very high development Time/costs for quality Scheduling
Teleconferencing	Interactive Immediacy Participatory	Complexity Unreliability Scheduling
Computer and Web-based learning	Interactive Learner controlled Participatory	High development Time/costs Equipment required Some unreliability

Selection of technology by distance teaching institutions for their management and instructional purposes depends on a number of factors.

There are a large number of technological options available for delivery of distance learning courses. A consistent problem through the history of distance education has been the tendency of educators to become fixed on a particular technology. The latest technology to capture attention is, of course, the internet and World Wide Web. What iss the most appropriate technology for delivering a specific course is a creative question. In setting up programmes and designing courses a basic principle is to recognize that each medium has its special strengths and weakness and these must be considered when deciding how to deliver each part of the course to its particular target population. The following summarises some of the strengths and weakness of the main technologies (Moore and Kearsley).

Bates provides the ACTIONS model for making decisions about the use of technology, suggesting that the factors to be considered can be summarised as follows:

A Access: Where will students learn; at home, or work or local centre?
C Costs: What are capital and recurrent; fixed and variable?

T Teaching functions: What are presentational requirements of the subject/Required teaching and learning approaches?
I Interaction: What kind of teacher and student interaction will be possible?
O Organization: What changes in organizations will be required to facilitate the use of particular technology?
N Novelty: Will the 'trendiness' of this technology stimulate funding and innovation?
S Speed: How quickly and easily can material bee updated and changed? How quickly can new courses be produced using this technology?

The selection and valid mix of technologies would depend on two kinds of contexts, i.e., environmental context and learning context. As environmental context is concerned, technology must be chosen in the light of criteria such as availability, accessibility, acceptability and economics. As learning context such as course objectives, assessment demands, subject matters and instructional strategies. This is shown in Fig. 22.1.

Bate's book *Technology, E-learning and Distance Education* is the essential guide for any one wanting advice on how to choose the right technology at the right cost for a course or flexible learning programme. One of the basic premise of this book is that newer technologies such as www are not necessarily better (or worse) for teaching or learning than older technologies such as print or video conferencing. New technologies are just different, and we need to understand the differences and the appropriate circumstances for applying various technologies for effective distance teaching and learning. The choice should be driven not by its novelty but by the needs of the learners and the context in which we are working.

Another premises is that lessons learned in the past from research into some of the older technologies are often still relevant for the newer technologies.

Another premises is that there is a direct link between the use of technology and different ideologies of teaching and learning. The effectiveness of a technology cannot be judged without making some basic assumptions about what constitutes effective teaching and learning and the goals and purpose of education and training.

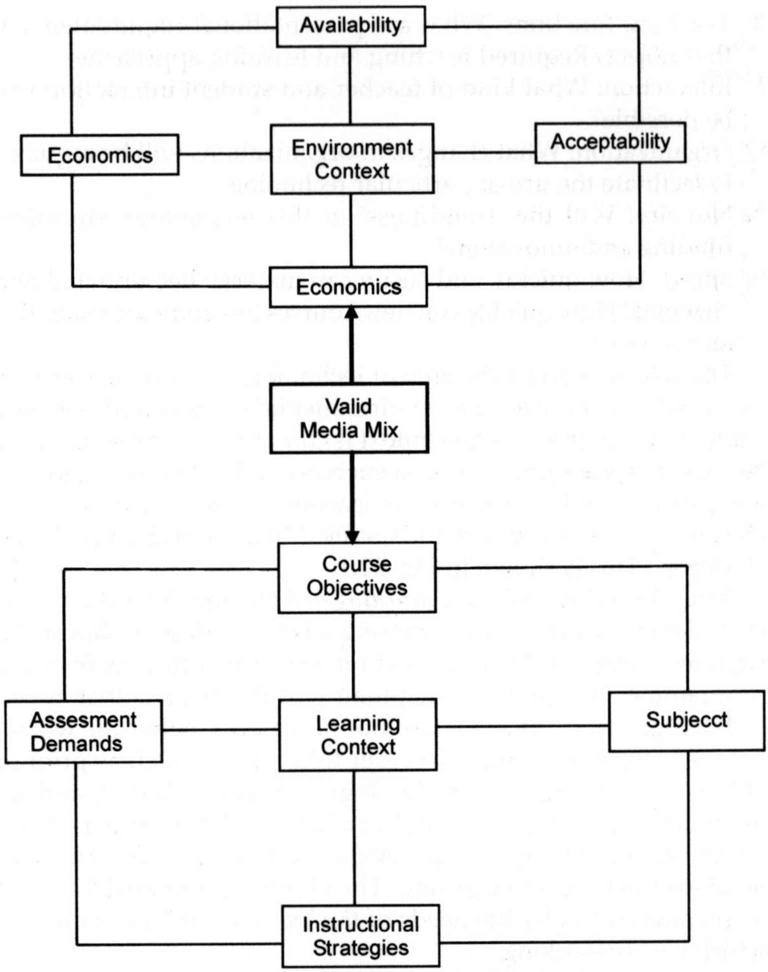

Fig 22.1: Selection of Valid Mix of Technologies

It is easy to be seduced by the excitement of the latest technology but technologies do not roll out evenly and all at once.

A feature of distance education institutions is that they are deliberately designed and structured to exploit the cost and educated benefits of technology.

Golden Rules for Technology Use in Education

Bates proposed twelve golden rules for using technology in

education and training that apply whatever technologies are used. These rules, given below are polpulary called golden rules.

1. Good teaching matters.
2. Good design essential.
3. Each medium has its own aesthetic.
4. Educational technologies are flexible.
5. There is no super technology.
6. Make all five media (face-to-face, print, audio, video, digital multimedia) available.
7. Interaction is essential.
8. Student numbers are critical.
9. New technologies are not necessarily better than old ones.
10. Team work is essential.
11. Teachers need training to use technologies effectively.
12. Technology is not the issue.

A distance education institution should consider these golden rules while selecting and using technologies for its distance teaching.

Use of Technologies in Indian Open and Distance Learning

Indian distance education institutions are presently making use of the following technologies for distance teaching students support and institutional management:

- Radio broadcasts
- Audio cassettes
- Audio conferencing
- Interactive radio phone-in-counselling
- TV broadcasts
- Video cassettes
- Video conferencing
- Computer associated management
- Computer mediated communications
- Computer conferencing
- Internet

Indian is one of the few developing countries that has made revolutionary strides in modernizing communication technologies. The first radio programme in India started in 1923 and educational use of radio began in 1930. The last three decades, in particular, have been very innovative, productive and imaginative with the development of TV, a new chapter has been added to the already widening circle of transmission systems. TV entered India five decades back in 1959 as a pilot project founded by the Ford Foundation. A significant landmark in the history of television in India was the one-year 'Satellite Instructional Television Experiment (SITE)' launched in August 1975. An American satellite was extensively used to telecast messages since the operationalization of INSAT-1B in 1983, television network started getting spread. From the very beginning, television has been perceived as a potential tool for imparting education as an agent for social change.

The development, transfer and adoption of new technologies are not as simple ass they appear. Various factors and forces influence the ease of using technologies in distance education. The problems involved in the use of technologies are multiple and critical in developing countries. The influencing factors can be categorized into five-political, economic, cultural, educational and technological. The level of technological infrastructure in a country greatly conditions the uses of technologies. India's level of technological infrastructure is low,. Despite this, technologies are used in distance education institutions in India, particularly University-level distance education institutions, the distance teaching universities or open universities offering courses through the face-to-face mode and distance mode.

Research on the Use of Technology in Indian Open Universities

A few research studies were conducted on the use of technology in some open universities in India. On B.R. Ambedkar Open University's use of technology four research studies, which were awarded Doctoral degrees, focused on the multimedia based instructional system of BRAOU. The researchers found several weaknesses in the system and made several suggestions, some of which are the following:

1. Induction meetings for newly admitted students every year should be held at study centres for orienting students on the usefulness of technology for student learning.
2. Student Handbooks/Programme Guides for all courses should include advantages of print and non-print technologies to students in their learning.

3. Academic counsellors and study centre coordinators should motivate the students towards the use of non-print electronic media programmes.
4. All radio broadcasts and television broadcasts of the University should be put on cassettes/tapes/CDs/DVDs, and be made available to students at study centres.
5. Maximum number of study centres should be quipped with the gadgets and services necessary for presentation of electronic media programmes. In view of the increasing role of technology in distance education, the following equipment needed to be placed at maximum number of study centres of the University, and maintenance should be given top priority:
    - Telephone
    - Telephone with STD facility
    - Mobile phone
    - Tape recorder
    - Radio cum tape recorder
    - TV set
    - TV set with cable connection
    - TV with DTH
    - TV with MANA TV reception facility
    - VCP/VCP/DVD player
    - Computer with interest facility
    - Scanner
    - Audio cassettes
    - Video cassettes
    - Fax machine
    - Xerox machine
    - Overhead/LCD projector
6. One Sundays and other holiday, study centre should conduct additional sessions especially for presentation of audio and video programmes.
7. Media production facilities at the University headquarters should be augmented in terms of technical personnel and modern equipment.
8. Interaction between academics, production staff and student support planners should be more and continuous.
9. Rational decision making on media components of courses should happen.
10. Proper coordination is required between AIR, Doordarshan, MANA TV and University on the role of media.
11. Training in media planning and production for academics, production staff should be periodically organized with the help of EMPC, AIR, Doordarshan, MANA TV and such other organizations.
12. Training the trainers like academic counsellors coordinators of study centre and course writers to orient them to distance education system should be given top priority.

23

Quality Assurance

Quality assurance is the systematic monitoring and evaluation of the various aspects of a project, service or facility to ensure that standards of quality are met. It is a set of activities or procedures that an organization undertakes to ensure that standards are specified and reached consistently for a product or service. From the above, it can be defined as a process of building in quality by carrying out a set of activities to ensure that set standards are met.

Quality has always been an issue in open and distance education. The Commonwealth of Learning defines quality assurance as approaches to organising work that:

- ensures the institution's mission and aims are clear and known to all;
- ensures the systems through which work will be done are well thought out and communicated to everyone;
- defines and documents the institution's sense of quality;
- sets in place systems to check that everything is working to plan, and
- when things go wrong and they will - there are agreed ways of putting them right.

Purposes of Quality Assurance

Quality assurance in open and distance education reflects international trends. It serves purposes (Bernadette Robinson):

- to satisfy the need for accountability for funds used;
- to ensure that defined standards will be reliably achieved and that awards have credibility;
- to inform decision making when setting standards or redefining goals;

- to demonstrate good practice;
- to impress quality and standards in programme provision, service delivery, operations, student learning and institutional performance;
- to provide reference points, internal and external, past and present, for judging performance;
- to provide evidence of achievement in relation to competitors;
- to gain public confidence; and
- to ensure that learners receive the programme and services as promised in programme information and at registration.

Challenges of Implementing QA in ODE

The challenge of implementing quality assurance in open and distance education institutions is a monumental task which demands a great deal of effort. Changing an organisations mindset is one of the biggest tasks when undergoing innovation. Such change requires a great deal of courage and commitment of the top leaders of an institution.

The quality assurance in open and distance education in the last two decades has become a very pervasive issue for regulatory agencies in education. The first collective effort in the matter was done in 1995, when ICDE organised a world conference. The main theme of this conference was how to solve the quality assurance issue in open and distance education. The higher education practitioners observed that there is an increased use of distance education in education sector as a result of which a large number of universities are changing their mode of study from face to face to open distance mode or adopting dual mode. Thus quality assurance has become a challenge for regulatory agencies.

Several different organizations from different countries have developed principles, guidelines or benchmarks to ensure quality of distance education. In the UK, new guidelines for distance learning in higher education have been published by the Quality Assurance Agency. The guidelines were arranged under sub headings: (1) System design, (2) Programme design, approval and review, (3) Management of programme delivery, (4) Student development and support (5) Student Communication and representation, (6) Student assessment. Each one deals with an aspect where quality assurance is likely to require attention in a particular way when study is by distance mode.

Organizational Differences in Quality Assurance Arrangements

Distance education has the following organizational differences which need to be addresses in quality assurance arrangements (Bernadette Robinson):

- More parties, stakeholders, specialists or sites involved in the development and delivery of a course or programme.
- More separate activities, roles and players to be coordinated.
- Longer chains of communication
- More detailed planning of production and budgets in advance of programme presentation.
- A greater number of administrative tasks and partners.
- More diverse target audiences, with differing needs to be met and provisions to be made.
- In some cases more electronic transactions.
- More complex arrangement for the assessment of practical work and its delegation to local or workplace agents and partners.
- A distinguished organizational structure in some cases, either in materials creation or teaching arrangements or in learner support.
- More frequent collaboration with other institutions or agencies for the delivery of a programme or course together with reliance on partners.
- A different interpretation of what constitutes teaching (the separation of roles in providing learning content, tutoring and assessment).

Accommodating these differences in quality assurance systems has been essential in enabling the credibility of open and distance learning.

Quality Assurance to be Integral Part of ODE

Quality assurance should therefore be an integral part of any open and distance education operational systems and processes. Since the inception of open and distance education programme and their subsequent widespread diffusion, they have been increasing considerably the access to education for many students seeking higher education and this reality has compelled many countries to adopt the distance education mode ass part of their educational systems. Hence, starting from 1990, quality assurance concerns in distance higher education have gained serious attention by institutions, stakeholders and scholars as a result of which many institutions have begun to redefine and reorient their institutional missions and strategic visions to incorporate and address quality issues. Numerous reports have been published to share ideas, experiences and articulate the implementation of best practices of quality assurance in distance educational contexts from around the world.

Quality Assurance Organizations

The rapid expansion of distance education has forced accreditation agencies and national, regional and international quality assurance bodies to develop criteria for the assessment of quality in open and distance education. National, regional and international initiatives are given below:

National Quality Assurance Bodies

- The Tertiary Education Quality and Standards Agency (Australia)
- Distance Education Bureau of UGC (India)
- Universities Academic Audit Unit (New Zealand)
- Quality Assurance Agency (United Kingdom)
- Council for Higher Education Accreditation (USA)
- Western Cooperative for Educational Telecommunications (USA)
- Distance Education Training Council (USA)
- South African Institute for Distance Education (South Africa)

Regional Quality Assurance Initiatives

- Caribbean Area Network for Quality Assurance in Tertiary Education (Caribbean)
- European Association for Quality Assurance in Higher Education (Europe)
- African Quality Assurance Network (Africa)
- Asian Association of Open Universities (Asia)
- Asian Pacific Quality Network (Asia)

International Organizations

- International Council for Open and Distance Education
- United Nations Educational, Scientific and Cultural Organization

- International Association of Universities
- Association of Universities and Colleges of Canada
- American Council on Education
- Council for Higher Education Accreditation

Initiatives on Quality Assurance

Various national, regional and international initiatives have been undertaken with regard to quality assurance in distance education, including e-learning. Examples are:

- UK Quality Assurance Agency's guidelines on the quality assurance of distance learning
- Norwegian Association for Distance Education's quality standards for distance education.
- Australian Council on Open, Distance and e-learning's Benchmarks for the distance education and e-learning.
- National Association of Distance and Open Education Organizations of South African Quality criteria for designing and delivering distance education.
- African Higher Education Quality Rating Mechanism.
- European Association of Distance Teaching Universities Manual for e-learning in Higher Education.
- Asian Association of Open Universities AAOU Quality Assurance Statements of Best Practice.

Quality Assurance Mega Universities

Insung Jung conducted a survey in 2004 to report quality assurance practices and issues in 8 mega universities. The mega universities surveyed have different types and levels of organizational structures and policies on quality assurance. Quality assurance structures in the mega universities are categorized into three types: a centralized quality assurance structure, a collective quality assurance structure, and a dispersed quality assurance structure. Quality assurance policies and regulations have been set in all the institutions surveyed. The survey showed that quality assurance in a most mega universities has similar objectives, but is assessed by a variety of instruments and methods. For most institutions, the main objectives are self-improvement and accountability to the society in general and to the National Quality Assurance Authority in specific. The mega universities have developed quality assurance criteria for key areas of distance education.

Detailed quality assurance criteria are provided for mega universities surveyed. Internal quality assurance systems of most of the surveyed institutions have been linked to the national quality assurance framework either for distance education or for higher education in general.

The survey results showed that a quality culture has been emerging in mega universities. All the mega universities have developed and implemented quality assurance standards and procedures in key areas of distance education activities.

Quality Assurance in Asian Distance Education

In 2011, quality assurance in Asian Distance Education was studied by a team of Insung Jung, Tat Meng, Chen Li, Sanjaa Bagand Tian Belwati. The study was funded by the Openness and Quality in Asian Distance Education Project from the International Development Research Centre of Canada. The study team analysed the present quality assurance frameworks in 11 Asian countries and found that the level of quality assurance policy integration in the overall national quality assurance in higher education policy framework varied considerably and that obvious commonalities underpinned different quality assurance efforts.

The study team found the following quality assurance regulatory agencies/units in the Asian country's distance education institutions.

Quality Assurance Regulatory Agencies/Units in Asian Countries

- China—Distance and Continuing Education Office of Higher Education Department of MOE.
- Hong Kong—Hong Kong Council of Accreditation of Academic and Vocational Qualifications.
- India—Distance Education Bureau of UGC.
- Indonesia—National Accreditation Board of Higher Education.
- Japan—
  1. National Institute of Academic Degree and University Evaluation
  2. Japanese University Accreditation Association.

  Korea—
  1. Korean Council for University Education.
  2. Korea Education and Research Information Service.

Malaysia—	Malaysian Qualifications Agency
Mangolia—	Mangolian National Council for Education Accreditation
Philippines—	1. Accreditation Association of Chartered Colleges and Universities of Philippines.
	2. Philippines Accrediting Association of Schools, Colleges and Universities.
Singapore—	MOE's Quality Assurance Framework for Universities.
Sri Lanka—	Quality Assurance and Accreditation Council of the UGC/Ministry of Education.

In the light of their findings, the authors suggested that the following 6 principles should underpin national quality assurance policy directions and that without them there would be a considerable waste of resources and human potential in Asian distance education:

- All nations should see quality assurance as an integral part of broader national, regional and international quality assurance frameworks.
- Concerted efforts are needed from governments, national and regional quality assurance bodies, and insinuations regarding cross border accreditation and quality assurance in Asian distance education.
- With the convergence of conventional and distance education methods, there should be no distinction between quality assurance in distance education and conventional higher education or between e-learning and face-to-face learning.
- Understanding the relative and value-laden nature of quality assurance, Asian governments, DE provides, and assessors should make an effort to understand distance learners' concerns and integrate their views when developing national and institutional quality assurance policies because the success of DE typically relies to a great extent on learners' motivation and engagement.
- The existence of national quality assurance frameworks would enable DE institutions to make quality assurance an integral part of their institutional missions with respect to teaching and research and to promote a culture of quality in their institutions.
- As COL and Shale and Gomes argue, quality key performance

indicators will help DE institutions monitor their performance
indicators will help DE institutions monitor their performance
against institutional objectives and key principles of their plan.

Overall, quality assurance is still at an early stage of developments compared with quality assurance in conventional higher education quality assurance in distance education is still relatively new concept in some countries and a different quality assurance approaches described above reflect the differences in cultures, expectations and stages of development. Each of these approaches has its own particular strengths and weaknesses, so it would be invidious to prescribe any single approaches. However it is suggested that certain policy directions based on strong research evidence should underpin national quality assurance systems.

24

Leadership

The continuing success and future of distance education depends on effective leadership. Creating a vision for the future, providing direction for the effective use of technology, managing ensuing change, supervising DE staff and guiding faculty in transitioning from face-to-face learning environment and using the right pedagogy requires effective leadership. Effective leadership requires the leader to understand, engage and care for followers and to enable these followers to maximise their contributions.

Today's higher education DE leader assumes many roles and acts as an intermediary between multiple internal and external constituencies; work in an evolving that is part of an old system; and operates in a fast changing environment.

Leadership in distance education is focused less in the literature on distance education. There is a wide gap in the research literature on distance leadership.

Beaudoin (2003) reviewed the literature which was published in the 1990s, by conducting a content analysis of: (1) the titles and abstracts that appeared in the American Journal of Distance Education, and DEOSNEWS, an electronic journal, both published by the American Center for the Study of Distance Education; (2) 1998 and 1999 issues of Open Learning; and (3) 1997-1999 issues of Distance Education, and founded only a few articles related to distance education leadership. He concluded that "over a four-year period, several widely read sources of research and writing in distance education theory and practice offer us very little indeed on the topic of leadership". Beaudoin also conducted content analysis of presentations at: (1) the European Distance Education Network, Bologna, Itlay (1998); (2) the Distance Education Conference, sponsored by the University of South Africa (2000);

and (3) the ICDE World Conference on Open Learning and Distance Education, held in Dusselddorf, Germany (2001), and found that "the interest and attention focused on the general theme of distance education management, in general, and leadership, in particular, was conspicuously thin".

The books devoted to open and distance education leadership and management are not many and included those of Dunning, Vankekrik and Zabrowski (1993); Freeman (1997);Paul (1990); Cynthia (1998); Latchem and Hanna (2001) and Beaudoin (2005).

Emerging leaders in distance education will need to be well versed in the business functions of their universities and colleges so that system and structures operate smoothly and effectively for students, faculty and support staff. The more to distance education requires that institutions effectively utilize business plans to a greater extent than many administrators are used to doing. It is evident from Floker's researches (2005) that emerging distance education leaders will not only need to be successful business managers but also need to understand concepts relating to the management of human capital.

Paul (1990), based on his experience, suggested that the following are the essential characteristics of strong positive leadership in distance higher education institutions:

- A clear vision for the organization and the ability to articulate it and inspire commitment to it.
- A passionate belief in the organization and the directions it is pursuing.
- A positive view of people, one holding that people can achieve if they are given the opportunity and support.
- Dedication to excellence and the unrelenting pursuit of the organization's goals.
- High self-esteem, and self-knowledge about both strengths and weaknesses, so as to capitalize fully on the former and to compensate for the latter by finding people who are excellent in these areas.
- A sense of humour, integrity and perspective that temper the strong leadership drive with sensitivity to colleagues and ability to lead a happy life, both on and of the job.
- A commitment to learning and change, first of all for his or her own lifelong development and secondly for the organization.

Leadership Styles in Asian Open Universities

Reardon (1995) classified leadership's styles into four types, as follows:

1. Commanding,
2. Logical,
3. Inspirational, and
4. Supportive

Leaders with a commanding style tend to 'take charge and make rapid changes'. Leaders with a logical style are more analytical, and carefully formulate plans for incremental changes. Leaders with an inspirational style are creative and empower others by inviting them to share visions. They introduce radical ideas and persuade others by creating trust. Leaders with supportive style want to please other people. They facilitate work, encourage openness and seek staff consensus in decision making. Zhang and colleagues conducted a survey on selected open universities in the Asian region, and characterized them on the Basis of Reardon's classification of leadership styles.

Leadership Styles in Selected Asia Open Universities (Zhang *et al.*, 2000)

Open University	*Country*	*Leadership Style*			
		Commanding	*Logical*	*Inspirational*	*Supportive*
RTVUs	China	3.16	3.20	3.15	3.15
OUs	India	3.54	3.28	3.25	3.41
OUHK	Hong Kong	3.13	2.90	3.25	2.27
KNOU	Korea	2.60	3.10	2.80	3.20
AIOU	Pakistan	3.20	2.80	2.90	3.10
STOU	Thailand	2.55	2.48	2.30	2.23
UPOU	Philippines	4.00	4.00	4.00	4.00
OUSL	Sri Lanka	2.88	2.98	2.90	3.10
BOU	Bangladesh	3.45	3.10	2.60	2.60
PNU	Iran	3.20	3.40	3.45	3.55
UAJ	Japan	3.30	3.40	3.00	3.00
NOU	Taiwan	3.50	3.30	2.90	3.50

Subjective ratings from (1) most important to (4) least important

Referring to the need for enlightened and effective leadership for distance teaching universities, Paul (1990) stated: "The success of open universities depends on leadership and vision- a value-driven commitment to the ideas of open learning, honesty and integrity without rigidity—a flexible approach in a world of ambiguity, change and challenge. If every institutional leader strives for open management, leadership which encompasses the values of open learning which we hold up for our students, the world's open universities will be much more effective institutions and will increasingly be seen as models for the universities of tomorrow".

Characteristics which Undermine Leadership

Paul (1990) offers the following behaviours or characteristics of leaders who are ineffective:

- Uncertainty or confusion about goals are directions
- Undue sense of self-importance whereby the so called leader treats colleagues as subordinates, and usually lacks the listening skills to sensitive and effective organizational leadership.
- Lack of a sense of humour
- Insincerity—trust is fundamental to the success of a leader and it can quickly be undermined by any of the following—giving different messages to different groups, participarting in catty gossip, or being openly manipulative in almost all dealings with people.
- Insecurity—it is almost impossible to convey a sense of direction and confidence if one is display in personal insecurities.

Emerging Distance Education Leaders

Emerging distance education leaders can be responsible for part or all of the dimensions and factors involving distance learning imitative. Depending on the scope and functions of a specific programme, a leader may need outside resources to maintain consistency. Simonson, Smaldino and Zvacek (2009) discuss Anthony Kaye's four subsystems of a distance education system that include all the regulatory subsystem, course subsystem, student subsystem and logistical subsystem. Within each of these categories exists a multitude of administrative and leadership functions. The authors outline a distance leader pyramid of competencies that include and have been listed top down as visioning, leading, managing, designing and knowing. Within these constructs, an emerging distance teacher must be knowledgeable in various areas such as policy, regulation, state and federal government influences, financial aid, copyright, data gathering, regional, national and professional accreditation, accessibility, intellectual property rights, faculty issues and finally, the costs and budgetary influences associated with distance learning agenda.

Leadership in a set of attitudes and behaviours that create conditions for innovative changes, enable individuals and organizations to share a vision and more in the appropriate direction and contribute to the management and operationlisation of ideas.

Emerging leaders in distance education not only must be transformational leaders but must also became situation leaders who are innovative visionaries that can motivate, energize, inspire, and induce others to more forward while fully articulating a shared and competitive distance learning agenda. Beaudoin (2002) states that emerging leaders in distance education need a variety of skills that are constantly refined and those include resource mobilization, needs assessment, fitting technology to needs, programme evaluation and accreditation, policy formulation, strategic planning, operationalising ideas, market analysis, implementing online infrastructure, collaborating with partners, training and support for faculty and mentoring the next generation of leaders. Simonson (2004) commenting on the distance learning leaders said:

> A distance learning leader is a visionary capable of action who guides an organization's future, its vision, mission, goals, and objectives. The leader guides the organization and its people who have faith in the leader and have a clear understanding and acceptance of the organization's worthwhile and shared vision and goals. A distance learning leader has competence in knowing, designing, managing, leading and visioning distance education.

25

Evaluation

The notion of evaluation has been around a long time. In addition to its long history, evaluation also has varied definitions and may mean different things to different people. Evaluation can be seen as synonymous with tests, descriptions, documents, or even management. Many definitions have been developed, but a comprehensive definition holds that evaluation is "systematic investigation of the worth or merit of an object."

This definition centers on the goal of using evaluation for a purpose. Accordingly, evaluations should be conducted for action-related reasons, and the information provided should facilitate deciding a course of action.

Why Evaluation?

There are two very important answers to this question. First and foremost, evaluation provides information to help improve the project. Information on whether goals are being met and on how different aspects of a project are working are essential to a continuous improvement process. In addition, and equally important, evaluation frequently provides new insights or new information that was not anticipated.

Over the years, evaluation has frequently been viewed as an adversarial process. Its main use has been to provide a "thumbs-up" or "thumbs-down" about a programme or project. In this role, it has all too often been considered by programme or project directors and coordinators as an external imposition that is threatening, disruptive, and not very helpful to project staff. While that may be true in some situations, evaluations need not be, and most often are not, conducted in an adversarial mode.

The goal of evaluation is to determine the worth or merit of some procedure, project, process, or product. Well-designed evaluations also provide information that can help explain the findings that are observed. In these days of reform, educators are continually faced with the challenges of evaluating their innovations and determining whether progress is being made or stated goals have, in fact been reached. Both common sense and accepted professional practice would suggest a systematic approach to these evaluation challenges. The role that evaluation to be addressed, and the resources available. It is best to think of evaluation not as an event, but as a process. The goal should be to provide an ongoing source of information that can aid decision making at various steps along the way.

Gooler suggested the following seven criteria which seemed to him to be particularly relevant to distance education:

- *Equality of opportunity*: The extent to which distance education contributes to equality of educational opportunities.
- *Access*: The extent to which distance education provides access to home-based adults.
- *Relevancy to needs and expectations*: The extent to which distance education provides opportunities and services that are regarded as being of priority to communicates in general, or to specific individuals, and particularly where there are a number of potential target audiences with differing needs.
- *Quality of the programme offering*: The quality of the educational materials and their content in comparison with traditional systems. The quality of design and the ease with which persons obtain access to the materials may also be considered.
- *Learner outcomes*: The extent to which students achieve the goals which are set for them, or which they set for themselves. A distinction can be made here between students who gain a formal qualification set by the university (such as a degree), and those who, while apparently dropping out mid-way through their studies, have in fact accomplished everything they want to do.
- *Cost-effectiveness*: The extent to which distance education programmes are cost-effective, involving a study of the relative cost of the programme vis-à-vis conventional programmes in terms of the unit cost per graduate, per student participating, or per credit-hour earned. Valid measures of effectiveness are, however, very difficult to obtain.
- *Impact*: The impact which the programme has on institutions, other programmes and individuals, and particularly the way

in which a distance education programme has influenced their goals, policies and directions; the extent to which traditional institutions or programmes are led to experiment with new media, or to-operate with distance-teaching institutions in the production of materials or courses; and the extent to which they may adjust their academic regulations to allow, for example, transferability of credit between the distance-teaching programme and their own programme. Finally, a distance education programme may have an impact on its students and on society as a whole-for example, by bringing an increased awareness of health care as a result of a particular course or series of courses, or by increasing awareness of the educational needs of adults.

- *Generation of knowledge*: The extent to which distance education contributes knowledge useful to a better understanding of the learning process.

Four Point Criteria of Kegan and Rumble

Keegan and Rumble appraised the successes or failure of nine DTUs over the decade 1971-80 using a four-point assessment scheme- (1) the quality of the learning achieved, (2) the quantity of learning achieved, (3) the status of the learning achieved and (4) the relative cost of the learning achieved. They did not deal with internal efficiency. Keegan recommended the four point evaluation for the overall evaluation of any distance teaching system.

The sub-criteria under each of the four main criteria used by Keegan and Rumble are as follows:

i) The quality of the learning achieved
   Under this heading are considered:
   - the success of the system in widening access, not just in terms of absolute numbers, but in attracting specific target groups;
   - drop-outs;
   - the quantity of the output relative to the input (the output/input ratio);
   - the time it takes to produce the output; and
   - the system's success in satisfying national local and individual needs.

To receive a satisfactory evaluation the instruction is required to achieve measurable success in: (i) the avoidance of avoidable drop-out; (ii) the number of successful students as a proportion of the number of students admitted; and (iii) the time it takes for students to achieve successful outcomes.

ii) The quality of learning achieved
Under this heading are considered:
- the quality of the learning materials provided by the distance system;
- the extent to which distance teaching is a suitable vehicle for educating students in certain subjects;
- the extent to which education is provided as opposed to instruction;
- the effectiveness of learning at a distance; and
- the 'inter subjectivity' of learning at a distance.

iii) The status of the learning achieved.
Under this heading are considered:
- the extent to which other educational institutions recognise the studies for credit transfer purposes;
- the acceptance of the degrees and diplomas awarded as qualifying students to go on to higher level studies;
- the recognition of the awards by employers, and
- the esteem in which the distance teaching institutions and their awards are held in the community at large.

The status of distance programmes can be measured and data collected for evaluation on the extent to which other educational institutions recognize the studies for credit transfer; the acceptance of the distance degrees for higher level studies; and the recognition of the awards by managers in competitive interviews for employment.

iv) The relative cost of the learning achieved
Under this heading are considered:
- the cost efficiency of distance universities relative to conventional universities or to other modes of internal operation which the distance universities could adopt;
- the cost effectiveness of distance universities relative to conventional universities—the concept of cost effectiveness tries to weigh the relative value o the outputs in qualitative terms;
- the cost benefits of distanced and traditional university

education, in which the costs of the education provided and the benefits (direct and indirect, financial and social) to the individual and society are taken into account; and
- the opportunity cost of education at a distance.

Other Criteria

There are other criteria by which activities and programmes of Distance Teaching Institutions could be evaluated. McIntosh, Kemmis, and Rumble are prominent among those who provided different criteria of assessment of effectiveness of distance education.

McIntosh emphasises formative evaluation, defined as evaluation that is conducted in conjunction with the development of a new educational programme with the aim of influencing that develops.

Kemmis suggest four levels of evaluation, (1) programme evaluation, concerning general institutional relationships, (2) curriculum evaluation, concerning the educational arrangements of whole curricula and particular courses, (3) evaluation of student, concerning the opportunities for learning created by a particular teaching/learning encounter, (4) students concerning the opportunities for learning created by a particular teaching/ learning encounter, and (5) students assessments, concerning the outcomes of student learning.

Rumble basing on Gooler's criteria but taking into account various criteria suggested by others provides an evaluative analysis of distance education institutions on the seven criteria: (1) access, (2) relevancy to needs and expectations, (3) quality of programmes offered, (4) learner outcomes, (5) effectiveness and efficiency, (6) impact, and (7) generation of knowledge.

Performance Indicators

In recent years considerable interest is developing in the development of performance indicators as an aid to educational management and as a means of assessing the overall performance of an institution. Many now feel that there should be a series of performance indicators that can be used in non profit making service organizations like distance teaching universities to measure the effective and efficient accomplishment of the expectations of the institution's constituencies. Sorenson and Grove who worked on 'Cost-outcome and Cost-effectiveness Analysis: Emerging Non Profit Performance, Evaluation Techniques' indicated several service performance indicators. Of these the significant ones are availability, awareness, acceptability, accessibility, appropriateness extensiveness, efficiency, effectiveness and outcomes benefits/ impacts. Rumble ably summarised each of these service performance indicators by applying to distance education.

The development of performance indicators has its roots in the dissatisfaction of the U.K. government, in the early eighties, regarding the effectiveness of its universities. This was first manifested in the form of a green paper (Department of Education and Science, 1985) on the Development of Higher Education into the 1990s which pressed for improved contribution from the educational sector in national economic development. It demanded that higher education should be more responsive to the requirements of the economy, try to obtain increased private funding and should not be heavily dependent on public funds, should display greater selectivity in the allocation of research funding, and should be more cost conscious managing its resources efficiently and effectively. A Steering Committee, set up by the Committee of Vice Chancellors and Principals, to examine the efficiency and effectiveness of universities, in its report (the Jarratt Report) recommended that reliable and consistent performance indicators needed to be developed. It suggested that a range of performance indicators should be developed covering both inputs and outputs and designed for use both within individual institutions and for making comparisons within institutions.

Performance indicators fall somewhere between general programme statistics and formative/summative evaluations. A performance indicator system is a collection of statistics that can be used to monitor the ongoing status of a programme against a set of targets and metrics. Going beyond descriptive statistics, performance indicators begin to provide information that can be measured against a set of goals and objectives. Indicator systems are typically used to focus policymakers, educators, and the public on: (1) key aspects of how an educational programme is operating, (2) whether progress is being made, and (3) where there are problems (Blank). Because performance indicators focus on tangible results, they often go beyond traditional reviews of programme expenditures and activity levels. In fact, the term "performance" underscores the underlying purpose of indicator systems, i.e., to examine a program's accomplishments and measure progress toward specific goals. Performance indicators provide a snapshot of accomplishments in selected areas, however, in contrast to evaluations, the information is limited and is unlikely to provide an explanation of why a project may have succeeded or failed.

Research studies include descriptive information and provide targeted in-depth exploration of issues, but differ along other dimensions. Instead of being intended for decision making, research efforts typically are designed to explore conceptual models and alternative explanations for observed relationships.

Performance Indicators as Applied to Distance Education

- *Availability*: Number and type of course, materials for sale or use, service available, range of media available.
- *Awareness*: Knowledge of DE system among user population (courses offered etc.)
- *Accessibility*: Hours of opening of local study centres, broadcast transmission hours, access media in the home.
- *Extensiveness*: Student enrolments against target numbers/quotas, number of users of special services, percentage use of media.
- *Appropriateness*: Demand for courses/service; mismatch between demand and availability.
- *Efficiency*: Cost per service per student per course etc.
- *Effectiveness*: Comparison of planned to actual; Percentage utilizing facility or service; graduate success in employment etc. budgeted to actual cost; planned total cost per-student course; planned to actual wastage rates.
- *Acceptability*: Demand for courses, number of complaints about course content or services, complaints about speed for service.
- *Outcomes/Benefits/Impacts*: Increased earning power of ex-students/graduates, benefits to society, local community, other educational institutions, etc.

Taking into consideration various criteria suggested by distance educators and writers, a set of criteria appropriate to Indian conditions to appraise the performance of Indian distance higher education systems with particular reference to open Universities is evolved by some Indian distance educators. The suggested criteria include:

- Relevancy to needs and expectations of people
- Availability of courses
- Extensiveness
- Quality of courses offered
- Effectiveness and efficiency
- Learner outcomes
- Access
- Impact
- Generation of knowledge

26

Distance Education Research

Research is a critical and creative activity undertaken on a systematic, disciplined basis and dedicated to increasing knowledge. The results of research take many forms. Research contributes to knowledge directly through discoveries or otherwise through innovative ideas and techniques, conceptual refinements or constructive critiques and syntheses which extend existing knowledge or its applications (Evans, Haminlton and Stokes). Open universities have many things in their favour, but generally research is not one of them. It has been argued that open universities have weak research performances in comparison with strong research universities. A reason may be the short history of open universities. One significant feature is that the open universities adopted institutional research as part of their tradition from the outset. Many open universities established around the world have developed significant institutional research units which contribute to quality research and scholarships in the field of open distance education. As observed by Evans (2000), there seems no doubt that the institutional research infrastructures in distance education organisations have been enormously influential in establishing research and scholarship in open and distance education. Institutional research produces multiple benefits for open universities. It enhances their practices, increase their research performance and help students establish their reputation as real universities.

Distance Education Study and Research Institutes, Centres and Divisions

Research in UKOU

Like other UK universities the OU actively engaged in research.

The OU Planetary and Space Sciences Research Institute has become particularly well known to the public through its involvement in space missions.

The OU employs over 500 people engaged in research in over 25 areas, and there are over 1200 research students. It spends about £20 million each year on research, around £ 6 million from the Higher Education Funding Council for England, the remainder from external funds.

The UK's latest Research Excellence Framework exercise (REF 2014) places the OU in the top third of UK higher education institutions by 'research power' ranking. 72 per cent OU research submitted was assessed as world-leading or internationally excellent.

The Open University has five research centres:

The Centre for Citizenship, Identies and Governance
The Centre for Research in Computing
The Centre for Research in Education and Educational Technology
The Centre for Earth, Planetary, Space and Astronomical Research
Open Space Research Centre

The OU is also partnered with other universities in two Economic and Social Research Council Centres:

The Centre for Social and Economic Research on Innovations in Genomics (with the University of Edinburgh)
The Centre for Research on Socio-cultural Change (with the University of Manchester)

Institute of Educational Technology

IET sets at the heart of the UKOU's pedagogy and research strategy, supporting the university as a visionary leader of educational technology. It champions open approaches to research, joins with world class researchers and links research and practice.

IET offers the following qualifications:

- Master in Online and Distance Education (also Certificate and Diploma)
- PhD programme in Educational Technology
- EdD Doctorate in Education

IET leads research into design and evaluation of teaching, learning and assessment with technology. Distinctive features are:

- Open approaches to research
- Co-design of new technology and innovative learning
- International Collaboration with world class researchers
- Linking research and practice

IET research is organised around three major themes:

- Leaning in an open world
- Innovating pedagogy
- Learning analytics

IET is involved in a number of research projects within these themes. IET research has a notable impact in open education, influencing professional practice and public policy.

IET delivers educational and professional development activities to enable staff to support the university's e-learning and e-teaching strategy.

IET's role is expanding following the Units recent move under the Pro-Vice Chancellor (Research, Scholarships and Quality).

Centre for Distance Education

Athabasca University has a Centre for Distance Education (CDE) led by a core faculty and supported by additional sessional instructors, offers graduate level courses and programmes that teach other educators how to develop, design and deliver online education. CDE is home to North America's first online Doctor of Education in Distance Education. It also offers a Master of Education in D/E and post-baccalaureate certificates and diploma in D/E technology. Institutional design and technology based learning.

Staff Training and Research Institute of Distance Education

Staff Training and Research Institute of Distance Education started as Division of Distance Education in 1986, soon after the establishment of IGNOU in 1985 to cater to the training needs of various functionaries of the Indira Gandhi National Open University (IGNOU).

Later, based on the proposal by Commonwealth of Learning (COL), the Asian Development Bank (ADB) and the Ministry of

Human Resource Development (MHRD), Government of India, the Division of Distance Education of IGNOU was upgraded into the Staff Training and Research Institute of Distance Education (STRIDE) in 1993.

STRIDE has been conducting training and research activities for IGNOU, State Open Universities (SOUs) and distance education institutes in India as well as serving the distance education training, research and capacity building needs of the Asian, African and the Caribbean countries (around 45 countries). More than 650 major training programmes have been conducted by STRIDE.

STRIDE offers M.A., M.Phil and PhD programme in Distance Education.

Research: STRIDE has been undertaking major research projects from time to time in areas of Course Design and Development, Student Persistence and Dropout, Cost Effectiveness, Job Market, Learner's Perception of ICT, Student Satisfaction, Evaluation of Training Activities and Academic Programmes.

Training Packages: STRIDE Develops training packages and other resource materials for training of various categories of functionaries working in the distance education system.

Staff Training and Capacity Building: STRIDE is entrusted with the responsibility of organizing capacity building and development programmes for teachers, academics and non-teaching staff members at the Headquarters and at the Regional Centres. STRIDE has conducted training programmes, workshops for teachers, academics and non-teaching staff of IGNOU, SOUs and DEIs and other institutions.

Indian Journal of Open Learning (IJOL): STRIDE is also looking after the Indian Journal of Open Learning (IJOL), a refereed/peer reviewed International Journal being published by IGNOU since 1992. The major objectives of this Journal are to disseminate information about theory, practice and research in the field of Open and Distance Learning (ODL), including multi-media distance education, educational technology and communication, independent and experiential learning and other innovative forms of education, and to provide a forum to researchers across the world to debate on these areas of concern with particular reference to the developing nations. The Journal is internationally contributed, subscribed and abstracted. From 1992 to 1996 IJOL was published twice a year and from 19997 onwards, it is published three times in a year.

G. Ram Reddy Research Academy of Distance Education

In order to benefit the Open Distance Learning systems of India and abroad, Dr. B.R. Ambedkar Open University has set up the GRADE. This Academy for research in distance education helps formalize and collate all academic efforts so as to encourage research studies in ODL system, which would not only greatly contribute for quality and development of distance education but also improve the services to the distance learners. The added benefit is that building a research environment is conducive to professional development of teachers of ODL and would certainly yield rich dividends to the open learning system.

The objectives of GRADE are:

- to carry out system-based research in distance education in India, the Asian Region and beyond;
- to conduct workshops, seminars and training programmes;
- to collaborate with institutions and agencies to undertake distance education research in India and abroad;
- to undertake consultancy;
- to sponsor research projects;
- to disseminate knowledge in the field of distance education;
- to establish and maintain a data bank in the field of distance education;
- to offer fellowships; and
- to conduct evaluation studies.

One of the important functions of the Academy includes organizing periodic interactive workshops on Research Methodology in Distance Education. Specific attention is given to impact studies, longitudinal studies and action research projects. It is also trying to build up data bases on different dynamics of ODL.

GRADE caters to the needs of distance teaching institutions, distance educators, researchers, policy makers, organizations and institutions with research interests for promoting distance education. Its specific functions are geared to match the requirements of target groups.

GRADE conducts evaluation studies on system and procedures adopted and student responses to various academic programmes, study material, and support services provided in order to get the feedback to improve the quality and relevance of programmes offered and services provided.

Research Institute of Open and Distance Education

Established in 1985 the Research Institute of Open and Distance Education of the Open University of China is China's oldest institute of DE in China. Since 2001 it became division of Open University of China.

Geared towards the interests of all OU students, the Institute actively pools the wisdom and talent of the experts and the staff members of OUs. Over the past 25 years, it has engaged in research and achieved numerous results in the theory and practice in such fields as distance education, open education, adult education, and the application of educational technology.

As the research arm of OUC, the Institute has undertaken numerous national level research projects since 1986. Such projects include the research on educational mode, curriculum design, teaching mode, administrative mode, support services, as well as quality assurance, and the assessment system of distance education. The research findings have been published in many journals and books. As a result of such sustained academic pursuits, a team of full-time and part-time researchers, which consists of researchers, teachers, administrators and technicians, has emerged. They have gained a solid domestic and international reputation for the quality of their research in distance education.

Since 2008, the Institute has been publishing, on an irregular basis, *Currents in Research* (internal circulation). The Journal focuses on the latest developments and trends in research in educational technology as well as in open and distance education (ODE). The articles may serve as the rationale and reference for decision-making, strategy planning, curriculum development, technology application, support services, and other research projects of the OUs throughout the country.

Currently, it consists of the Division of Theory and Policy Studies, the Division of Teaching and Management Studies, the Division of Media Technology and Application Studies, the Research Management Office, and the Administrative Office.

The Institute, established in 2001, is mainly responsible for the planning, administration, and designing of the research projects; for the organization, submission, approval, administration, and inspection of the research projects of OUC; for the organization, coordination and approval of submission of the research projects that are funded by various sources; for the publication and promotion of the research findings; and the provision of research-related information and related services. In the meantime, it supervises and coordinates the research activities among all OUs in China. Through research projects and academic activities that it sponsors, the Institute provides researchers with a platform for academic exchanges.

The Institute, as the member of the CAHE (Chinese Association of Higher Education), the College Distance Education Committee of the Chinese Educational Technology Association, and the secretariat of the Pedagogical Reform Committee of the Chinese Adult Education Association, also exercises the responsibilities of organization, liaison, coordination and day-to-day work of these associations and committees.

University Research Centre

University Research Centre is the centralised unit of the Open University of Hongkong, overseeing research activities of the Open University of Hongkong, coordinating and supporting research carried out by staff of the Open University of Hongkong. It was transformed in 2012 from the Centre for Research in Distance and Adult Learning which was setup in 1997.

The International Research Foundation for Open Learning

The International Research Foundation for Open Learning (IRFOL), which was set up in the UK in 1955, has now ceased to trade as a separate organisation and its website is no longer available. It was closed in March 2011.

IRFOL was an independent research agency that studied world-wide changes to open and distance learning. In the 15 years of its existence IRFOL established an excellent track record and reputation for independent policy-oriented research on open and distance learning, and the application of information and communication technologies to education. Its work focussed mainly on higher education, basic education and the education and training of teachers in both industrialised and developing countries.

Several of its previous key staff members are still working as individuals and in teams and are undertaking research and consultancy in a variety of different countries.

Those continuing to be active include:

- Ros Morpeth
- Hilary Perraton
- Roger Mills
- Charlotte Creed

Distance Education Journals

Most of the research studies in distance education find place in distance education journals given below:

- *Asian Journal of Distance Education*
- *American Journal of Distance Education*
- *Canadian Journal of Learning Technology*
- *Distance Education*
- *European Journal of Open Distance and e-Learning*
- *Indian Journal of Open Learning*
- *International Review of Research in Open and Distributed Learning*
- *Journal of Distance Education*
- *Journal of Open, Flexible and Distance Learning*
- *Journal of Learning for Development*
- *Journal of Open, Distance and e-Learning*
- *Malaysian Journal of Distance Education*
- *Open Learning*
- *Open Proxis*
- *Turkish Online Journal of Distance Education*

Growth of Distance Education Research

The bulk of research in distance education derives from three sources:

Strong institutions with large research units, scattered individuals with special interest in the field, and specially funded major projects. In 1985 Moore reviewed the distance education research literature of the past twenty years and commented: the condition of research in distance education is about what might be expected at the early stage in the growth of a new field of education". Whereas, five years later Coldway (1990) stated that distance education research is not planned, consolidated and reported in a systematic manner. Now, the situation is different. Distance education research has matured.

Calvert (1986) discussed distance education research literature under the following heads:

a) students and curricula,
b) learning at a distance,
c) teachers at a distance,
d) learner support services,
e) technology for instruction,
f) institutional structure,
g) economics

in the recent years, research has been conducted to investigate distance education research trends. One of the first studies to investigate trends in distance education was carried out by Berge and Mrozowski (2001) who examined research literature over a ten year period from 1990 to 1999.

Lee, Driseall and Nelson (2004) also examined research topics methods and citation trends in four journals: The American Journal of Distance Education, the Journal of Distance Education, Distance Education, and Open Learning.

383 articles were selected and classified into six themes: design related, development related, management related, evaluation related, institutional and operational related and theory and research related.

A series of studies were conducted by Zawacki—Richter to explore research domain. The first study (2009) used a Delphi technique to develop a classification of research areas as shown below:

I. *Macro level*: Distance evaluation systems and theories
  1. Access, equity, and ethics
  2. Globalization of education and cross-cultural aspects
  3. Distance teaching systems and institutions
  4. Theories and models
  5. Research methods in distance education and knowledge transfer

II. *Meso level:* Management, organization and technology
  1. Management and organization

2. Costs and benefits
3. Educational Technology
4. Innovation and change
5. Professional development and faculty support
6. Learner support services
7. Quality assurance

III. *Micro level:* Teaching and learning
1. Instructional design
2. Interaction and communications
3. Learner characteristics

Aras Bozkurt, Sibel Yilnazar, Emel Guler and their associates explored the current trends in the field of distance education research during 2009-2013 by extensive review of seven peer revived scholarly journals. The review presented the current situation and provided a research direction for future research. Regarding the result as of study, the following implication can be considered for future researches:

- The term 'open and distance learning' is a better name for our field of study since it reflects the core assumptions of the field: openness, accessibility, flexibility, massiveness, and quality learning opportunities to all.
- The studies should not focus on only general characteristics of the learners, but also various individual differences including cognitive processes, learning strategies, cultural differences.
- Studies are needed which examine the learning processes in informal, non-formal learning environments as well as OERs and MOOCs to be able to provide better learning opportunities.
- A variety of research designs and models may be used to understand and to delve more deeply into the area. Especially mixed designs might helps scientific development of the field.

Minnis summarised research in distance education as follows:

- "most research remains overwhelmingly descriptive. The focus is narrow with emphasis on particular institutional problems;
- as a consequence of its problem solving orientation;
  research reflects an a historical and/or a theoretical bias, ignoring the need for theory construction;
- research tends to be context specific, that is few generalisations can be made beyond the specific population or sample studies;

- research looks meaningful, cross-cultured or comparative perspectives;
- the vast majority of research is heavily dependent on psychological paradigms"

Therefore, Minni recommended three methods - ethnography, case studies and grounded theory.

Saba and Twitchell identified four methods of enquiry for various functions of distance education system:

- Descriptive analysis to show how distance education systems are organised,
- Cost-benefit analysis to study financing and budgeting of systems,
- Survey methods to study utilisation patters and user attitudes towards the system, and
- Experimental research methods to study learners and to measure learning outcomes.

Mishra critically analyses 361 papers published in four leading journals and found that 47.64 percent of papers were descriptive in nature.

Areas of Research Priority in Distance Education

Marland (1989) identified six main areas that invite research attention. Taylor (1989) with specific reference to South Asia listed six areas as priority areas. Panda (1992) listed five important broad research areas needing urgent attention.

In a review of research on distance education in Norway, Rekkedal (1993) identified ten areas for research.

The most comprehensive listing of research areas was indicated by Moore (1989) in his editorial to American Journal of Distance Education based on the proceedings of the 'Distance Education Symposium: A Research Agenda'. The broad areas indentified are:

- Research on policy and administration
- Research on instruction
- Research on course design
- Research on learners and learning

On the basis of a survey two staff members of IGNOU suggested the following:

- Distance education practitioners should be encouraged to undertake research to accelerate the growth of distance education as a discipline.
- Researchers should be encouraged to collaborate with other disciplines to facilitate the branching out of distance education to other forms of study
- Research in distance education should not only focus on theoretical aspects but also on practical aspects so that research results can be used to solve the problem encountered
- Researchers should be given appropriate administrative support to conduct research

Howell, Williams and Lindsay identified 32 trends under 6 heads in distance education literature. According to them, any of these trends could be the subject of a research study:

- Student Enrolment Trends (5)
- Faculty Trends (9)
- Academic Trends (9)
- Teaching Trends (3)
- Economic Trends (3)
- Distance Education Trends (5)

Following are some of the broad areas on which research needs to be promoted intensively and immediately:

- politico-socio-economic factors influencing the decision making on distance education institutions.
- planning process for the establishment of distance education institutions
- advantages and disadvantages of distance education institutions in comparison with conventional institutions of education.
- national educational policies and their effects on distance education developments.
- Distance courses- types, planning, relevance, utility etc.
- identification of educational needs and demands—methods and mechanisms.
- offering science and technology courses—problems in providing lab facilities, practical works
- different approaches to the organization and management of the development and production of instructional materials.

- multimedia instructional systems—nature, components and problems.
- communication and information technologies—their role and application in distance education.
- student support services—Why? What? How? characteristics of learners—scio-economic—cultural—educational backgrounds.
- feedback from students on courses, tutoring and counselling and ways of obtaining and use. Problems of dropout and persistence—models of attrition evolved by Brindley, Bean and Metzner. Tinto, Wooddley and Parleett, etc., and their application and adoption.
- face to face tuition and correspondence tuition—purposes, functions and problems.
- regional and study centres—structure, functions and problems.
- mobile study centres—nature, operation and use.
- student assessment procedures and methods.
- performance indicators—development and application.
- impact of distance education institutions on conventional institutions and co-distance education institutions.

Annexure

Open Universities

Country	*Open University*
Australia	Open Universities Australia
Bangladesh	Bangladesh Open University
Canada	Athabasca University
China	Open University of China
Cyprus	Open University of Cyprus
Germany	Fern Universitat
Greece	Hellenic Open University
Hongkong	Open University of Hongkong
India	Indira Gandhi National Open University
India	B.R. Ambedkar Open University
India	Nalanda Open University
India	Vardhaman Mahaveer Open University
India	Yashwantro Chavan Maharashtra Open University
India	M.P. Bhoj University
India	Babasaheb Ambedkar Open University
India	Karnataka State Open University
India	Netaji Subash Open University
India	Rajashre Tandon UP Open University
India	Tamil Nadu Open University
India	Pt. Sundarlal Sharma Open University
India	Uttarakhand Open University
India	Krishna Kant Handique State Open University
India	Global Open University
India	Venkateshwara Open University
Indonesia	Universitas Terbuka
Iran	payame Noor University
Iran	Al-Mustafa Open University
Israel	Open University of Israel

Country	*Open University*
Japan	Open University of Japan
Jordan	Al-Quds Open University
Korea	Korea National Open University
Kuwait	Arab Open University
Libya	Open University of Libya
Malaysia	Open University of Malaysia
Malaysia	Wawasan Open University
Mauritius	Open University of Mauritius
Netherlands	Open University of Netherland
Nigeria	National Open University of Nigeria
Pakistan	Allama Iqbal Open University
Philippines	University of Philippines Open University
Portugal	Universidad Aberta
Sri Lanka	Open University of Sri Lanka
South Africa	University of South Africa
Spain	National Distance Education University
Spain	Universitat Oberta de Catalunya
Sudan	Open University of Sudan
Taiwan	National Open University of Taiwan
Tanzania	Open University of Tanzania
Thailand	Sukhothai Thammathirat Open University
Turkey	Anadolu University
U.K.	Open University
Vietnam	Hanio Open University
Vietnam	Ho Chi Minh City Open University
Venezuela	Open University of Venezuela
Zambia	Zambian Open University
Zimbabwe	Zimbabwe Open University

References

Bates, A.W. (ed.) (1990). *Media and Technology in European Distance Education.* Heerlen: EADTU.

Bates, A.W. (2005). *Technology and E-Learning and Distance Education.* London: Routledge.

Beaudian, M.F. (2003). Distance Education Leadership for the New Century. *Online Journal of Distance Learning Administration, 6(2).*

Beaudian, M.F. (2005). *Reflections on Research, Faculty and Leadership in Distance Education.* Olumberg: Bibliothecks.

Bell, R. and Malcolm, T. (1993). *Open Universities: A British Tradition?* Bristal: Society for Research into Higher Education.

Berge, Z. and Mrozowski, S. (2001). Review of Research in Distance Education. *American Journal of Distance Education, 15(3).*

Bozkurt, A. *et al.,* (2015). Trends in Distance Education Research: A Content Analysis of Journals 2009-2013. *The International Review of Research in Open and Distance Learning.*

Carty, W. (1999). Distance Education in the Developing World. *The Advising Quarterly,* Summer.

COL (1990). *Report on Round Table on Training in Distance Education.* Vancouver: COL.

Daniel, J.S. (1996). *Mega Universities and Knowledge Media.* London: Kogan Page.

Daniel, J.S. (1995). *Open Universities and the Knowledge Media: New Opportunities, New Threats.* A Paper to IX AAOU Conference.

Darojat, O., Nitson, and Kufman, D. (2015). Quality Assurance in Asian Open and Distance Learning: Policies and Implementation. *Journal of Learning for Development,* 2(2).

Dhanarajan, G. (1996). *Setting Up Open Universities.* British Council Seminar. Vancouver: COL

Dodd, J and Rumber, G. (1984). Planning New Distance Teaching Universities. *Higher Education, 13.*

Dhanarajan, G. (2001). Distance Learning: Promise, Performance and Potential. *Open Learning, 16(1).*

Ferguson, J. (1975). *The Open University from Within.* London: University of London.

Freeman, R. (2004). *Planning and Implementing Open and Distance Learning for Decision Makers.* Vancouver: COL.

Freeman, R. (2004). *Planning and Implementing Open and Distance Learning for Decision Makers.* Vancouver: COL.

Freeman, R. (1977). *Managing Open Systems.* London: Kogan Page.

Grint, K. (1977). *Leadership: Classical, Contemporary and Critical Approaches.* Oxford: Oxford University Press.

Guri Rosenblit, S. (1999). *Distance and Campus Universities: Tensions and Internactions.* Oxford: Pergnmon.

Harris, D. (1987). *Openness and Closure in Distance Education.* London: Falmer Press.

Harry, K. (ed.) (1989). *Higher Education through Open and Distance Learning.* London: Routledge.

Holmberg, B. (1989). *Theory and Practice of Distance Education.* London: Routledge.

Horlock, J. (2006). *An Open Book: A Memoir.* Weardale: The Memoir Club.

Horlock, J. (1984). *The Open University After 15 Years.* Proceedings of the Manchester Statistical Society.

Jegede, O. and Shive, G. (2001). *Open and Distance Education in the Asia and Pacific Region.* Hong Kong: OUHK Press.

Jung, I.S. (2004). *Quality Assurance and Accreditation Mechanisms of Distance Education for Higher Education in the Asia—Pacific Region: Select Cases.* University Workshop: Beijing.

Jung, I. *et al.*, (2011). Quality Assurance in Asian Distance Education: Diverse Approaches and Common Culture. *International Review of Research in Open and Distance Learning, 12 (6).*

Kaye, D. and Rumble, G. (1981). *Distance Teaching for Higher and Adult Education.* London: Croom Helm.

Keegan, D. (1996). *Foundations of Distance Education.* London: Routledge Falmer.

Kember, D. (1995). *Open Learning Courses for Adults.* Englewood Cliffs NJ: ET Publications.

Koul, B.N. and Kanwar, A. (ed.) (2006). *Perspectives on Distance Education: Towards a Quality of Culture.* Vancouver: COL.

Latchem, C. and Hanna, D. (2001). *Leadership and Management in Open and Flexible Learning.* London: Kogan Page.

Ljosa, E. (1980). Some Thoughts on the State of Research in Distance Education. *Distance Education, 1.*

Mace, J. (1978). Mythology in Making: Is the Open University really Cost Effective? *Higher Education, 19(3).*

Majdalawi, A. (2005). Distance Higher Education in Arab Region. *Online Journal of Distance Learning, VIII (1).*

Manjulika, S. and Reddy, V.V. (1999). *Unexplored Dimensions of Open Universities.* New Delhi: Vikas Publishing House.

Marland, P. (1989). An Approach to Research on Distance Learning. *British Journal of Educational Technology, 20(3).*

Mason, J. and Goodough, S. (1981). Course Creations. In A. Kaye and G. Rumble (eds) *Distance Teaching for Higher and Adult Education.* London: Croom Helm.

Mishra, S. (1998). Distance Education Research: A Review of its Structure, Methodological Issues and Priority Areas. *Indian Journal of Open Learning, 7(3).*

Mishra, S. (1997). A Critical Analysis of Periodic Literature of Distance Education. *Indian Journal of Open Learning, 6 (1 and 2).*

Mills, R. and Tait, A. (1996). *Supporting the Learner in Open and Distance Learning.* London: Pitman.

Moore, M.G. (1985). Some Observations on Current Research on Distance Education. *Epistoldidaktika, 1.*

Moore, M.G. and Anderson, W.G. (ed.) (2003). *Handbook of Distance Education,* Mahwah: Erlbaum.

Moore, M.G. and Thompson, M. (1990). *The Effects of Distance Education: A Summary of the Literature.*

Mugridge, I. (ed.) (1997). *Founding the Open Universities.* New Delhi: Sterling.

Neil, M.W. (ed.) (1981). *Education of Adults at Distance: A Report of the Open University Tenth Anniversary International Conference.* London: Kogan Page.

Nembiakkim, R. and Mishra, S. (2010). Distance Education Research: Attitudes and Barriers. *Indian Journal of Open Learning, 19(3).*

Paul, R.H. (1990). *Open Learning in Open Management: Leadership and Integrity in Distance Education.* London: Kogan Page.

Panda, S., Venkaiah, V. Garg, S., and Puranik, C. (2006). *Four Decades of Distance Education in India: Reflections on Policy and Practice.* Viva Books: New Delhi.

Perry, W (1976). *Open University: A Personal Account by the First Vice-Chancellor.* Milton Keynes: The Open University.

Nworie, J. and Oprandi, S. (2012). Leadership in Distance Education: Qualities and Qualifications sought by Higher Education Institutions. *American Journal of Distance Education, 26(3).*

Nworie, J. (2012). Applying Leadership Theories to Distance Education Leadership. *Online Journal of Distance Learning Administration, 15(5).*

Perraton, H. and Lentell (2004). *Policy for Open and Distance Learning.* London: Routledger Falmer.

Perraton, H. and Hulsmann, T. (1998). *Planning and Evaluating Systems of Open and Distance Learning.* Sheffield: Dept. For Education and Employment.

Peters, O. (2001). Learning and Teaching in Distance Education. London: Kogan Page.

Potashinik, M. and Capper, J. (1998). Distance Education: Growth and Development. *Finance and Development, 35 (1).*

Ram Reddy, G. (1987). Planning, Management and Monitoring of Distance Education. In *Distance Education in Asia and Pacific. Vol. I.* Manila: Asian Development Bank.

Ram Reddy, G. (ed.) (1992). *Open Universities: The Ivory Towers Thrown Open.* New Delhi: Sterling.

Reddi, U.V. and Mishra, S. (ed.) (2005). *Perspectives on Distance Education: Educational Media in Asia.* Vancouver: COL.

Robinson, B. (1981). Support for Student Learning. In A. Kaye and G. Rumble (ed). *Distance Teaching for Higher and Adult Education.* London: Croom Helm.

Rumble, G. and Harry, K. (ed.) (1982). *The Distance Teaching Universities.* London: Croom Halm.

Rumble, G. (1986). *The Planning and Management of Distance Education.* London: Croom Helm.

Rumble, G. (1992). *The Management of Distance Learning Systems.* Paris: UNESCO.

Rumble, G. (1992). The Competitive Vulnerability of Distance Teaching Universities. *Open Learning, 7.*

Sargent, N. *et al.*, (1989). *An Evaluation of the AIOU.* Islamabad: AIOU/ODA.

Satyanarayana, P., and Sesharatham, C. (2000). *Distance Education: What? Why? How?* Hyderabad: Book Links Corporation.

Satyanarayana, P., Sesharatnam, C., and Emmanuel D.K. Meduri (2015). *Distance Education: Origin, Growth and Development.* Delhi: Shipra Publications.

Sesharatnam, C. (2002). *India's First Open University.* Hyderabad: Book Links Corporation.

Schon, D. (1983). *The Reflective Practitioners: How Professionals Think in Action.* New York: Basic Books.

Simpson, O. (2000). *Supporting Students in Open and Distance Learning.* London: Kogan Page.

Shoemaker, C.J. (1998). *Leadership in Continuing and Distance Education in Higher Education.* Boston: Allyn & Bacon.

Taylor, J.C. (2001). *Fifth Generation Distance Education.* 20th World ICDE Conference, Germany.

Tunstall, J. (ed.) (1974). *The Open University Opens.* London: Routledge and Kogan Page.

UNESCO (2001). *Distance Education in E-9 Countries.* Paris: UNESCO.

UNESCO (2002). *Open and Distance Learning: Trends, Policy and Strategy Considerations.* Paris: UNESCO.

UNESCO-ROEAP (1985). Working Group Meeting on the Use of Advances in Communication Technology for Higher Education Purposes. Bangkok.

Weinbren, D. (2015). *The Open University: A History*. Manchester: Manchester University Press.

Willem, B. (1988). What Happened to the Open University Briefly? *Distance Education*, 9.

Wolf, H.D. (1986). The Main Features of the Dutch Open University. In G.V. *et al.*, (ed) *Distance Higher Education and the Adult Learner*. Heerlen: DOU.

Zawacki Richter, O. *et al.*, (2009). Review of Distance Education Research (2000 to 2008): Analysis of Research Areas, Methods and Authoring Patterns *International Review of Research in Open and Distance Learning, 10(6)*.

Zawacki Richter, O. (2009). Research Areas in Distance Education: A Delphi Study. *International Review of Research in Open and Distance Learning, 10(3)*.

Zhang, W.Y., Tsui, C. Jegede, O., Kwok and Ng, F. (2000). *A comparison of Distance Education in Selected Asian Open Universities. Proceedings of 14th AAOU Conference.* Manila: Philippines.

Index